More FOOD *for* FLATTERS

Tableware kindly supplied by

ISBN: 978-1-86971-121-4

First published in 2007 by Hodder Moa
Reprinted 2010, 2013

Reprinted in 2014, 2016
by Hachette New Zealand Ltd
Level 2, 23 O'Connell Street, Auckland, New Zealand

Text © Goodman Fielder New Zealand Limited 2007
The moral rights of the author have been asserted.
Design and format © Hachette Livre NZ Ltd 2007

All rights reserved. No part of this publication may be reproduced or transmitted in any form or by any means, electronic or mechanical, including photocopying, recording, or any information storage and retrieval system, without the permission in writing from the publisher.

Designed and produced by Hachette NZ Ltd
Cover design by Seymour Designs
Text and food styling by Sally Cameron
Photographs by Charlie Smith
Printed by Everbest Printing Co. Ltd

contents

Introduction	4
Setting up a kitchen	6
Feeding your flat on a budget	9
Grow your own ingredients	13
Weights and measures	15
Breakfast and brunch	**18**
Snacks and starters	**27**
Salads	**36**
Soups	**46**
Quick pasta and rice	**53**
Main meals with meat	**62**
Beef	64
Lamb	73
Pork and bacon	80
Chicken	85
Fish and shellfish	**93**
Vegetarian dishes	**101**
Desserts	**111**
Cakes and baking	**121**
Party food	**132**
Index	141

Introduction

For most New Zealanders the name 'Edmonds' is associated with reliable ingredients that are 'sure to rise', and a cookbook that has become a virtual Kiwi icon. The first edition of the *Edmonds Cookery Book* was published nearly 100 years ago, and for the best part of a century Edmonds has maintained its reputation for presenting tasty, everyday recipes that are easy to prepare.

Now the Edmonds team has brought together an exciting range of recipes that are geared towards the growing number of New Zealanders that choose to go flatting. Cooking with or for flatmates can be a challenging experience and one that is guaranteed to put both the imagination and the wallet to the test. The average flatting kitchen may lack the latest utensils and equipment, the shopping list may be seriously constrained by the weekly budget, and the level of the collective cookery skills may be at the 'early development' stage. However, none of this need deter the flatter who wants to eat well every day and even impress friends and family on the odd special occasion.

More Food for Flatters not only provides a wide selection of delicious ideas for meals and snacks. It also contains practical advice on how to make the most of the flatting kitchen – what basic utensils are needed, what ingredients to keep regularly in the pantry and how to organise the kitchen space to ease the pressure when preparing a meal.

It includes an easy-to-follow section on understanding food, which promises to be a much-used reference for the relative novice to cooking, and even for the more advanced chef. Ingredients, both the essential and not-so-ordinary, are explained and there are also handy suggestions of what to use when you run out of a key item.

More Food for Flatters will guide you through the trickiest culinary situations and provide you with essential cooking skills – from knowing how to cook pasta and rice to perfection, to ensuring meat is always cooked just to your taste, to providing your party guests with tasty nibbles and delicacies. Scattered throughout the book are creative tips to help save time and money, boost confidence and set even the most inexperienced cook on a path to expertise in the kitchen.

Over 150 easy-to-prepare recipes in the trusted Edmonds style cater for all meals and occasions, from breakfast and brunch, snacks and salads, soups and starters to pasta and rice. The culinary tastes and dietary preferences of all flatmates are catered for in the chapters on main meals with meat, fish and shellfish and vegetarian dishes. Those flatters with a sweet tooth will really enjoy the chapters devoted to desserts and cakes and baking. The 'Party food' section presents both innovative and traditional recipes that will allow the flatting cook to impress their guests with their style and skill.

Edmonds continues to provide New Zealanders with a core repertoire of culinary skills and recipes. *More Food for Flatters* is destined to become a must-have in all flatting kitchens, combining as it does fresh and funky recipes with great presentation ideas and good old-fashioned advice. We hope you enjoy cooking from this book.

The Edmonds Team

Setting up
a kitchen

Create a clean and safe space
Give your kitchen a good clean-out when you first move in and then on a regular basis. A good detergent, degreaser and some hard scrubbing can make any surface hygienic. Clean the oven, fridge and freezer inside and out. Make sure any mould or food scraps are completely removed. Clean the cupboards and floors and if necessary scrub the walls and ceiling. Dusty spaces aren't hygienic. If necessary, and if you are allowed, paint the walls and ceiling. White paint can hide a multitude of sins and create a clean and bright work area.

An efficient kitchen
Always double-check that the equipment in your flat or rented house runs well. A landlord may be uncooperative if you explain after the takeover period that the oven doesn't work or the cupboard doors are ready to fall off. Make sure this is all sorted before you sign the lease. Money can be saved on your power bills if the fridges run properly and there are no broken seals. Check any temperature fluctuations in the oven as well, using an oven thermometer.

Organise your kitchen

A small kitchen needn't be a drag if it is well organised. Plan where things are meant to go. Keep foods that are used most often in an accessible area, and pantry or bulk items tucked away. Sort out your fridge and utilise areas in the fridge that are the coldest for keeping meats and the most perishable of items. Use compartments for what they are designed for, such as vegetables or dairy products.

Keep it clean and tidy

Clean the kitchen on a regular basis. Don't let food sit and rot in the fridge or weevils breed in the pantry. Wipe out cupboards with plates and glasses and keep the cutlery drawer free of crumbs and spills. Any broken plates, chipped glasses or redundant equipment should be thrown out with the inorganic recycling. Bacteria easily breeds in cracks and crevices and appliances that are not used any more. If you don't need it get rid of it.

Clean as you go. Wipe benches, cupboards, sinks and window sills every day. It is amazing how much food, dust and mould can build up in this busy room. Have a place for everything and everything in its place, it makes the cooking process so much more streamlined. Try not to leave sharp knives in the bottom of messy cutlery drawers, they are dangerous and become blunt quicker. Space-saving devices such as racks and baskets work well to keep work surfaces clear and implements within easy reach.

Recycle

Set your kitchen up to handle recycling. Plastic buckets under the sink can divide food scraps from inorganic materials. Paper and plastic can be put directly into recycling bins and the vegetable scraps can be put into a small compost bin if you have got one going in your garden. Inorganic collections can pick up disused equipment and any hazardous chemicals can be disposed of via special council collections.

Equipment

Take care of your equipment. The better you look after it the longer it will last. Spend a few extra dollars on buying good-quality equipment items such as pots and knives and they will reward you in the long run with longevity and great culinary results.

For a list of equipment for your first flat or rented abode see *Food For Flatters*.

Setting up a kitchen

Basic hygiene and safety

- Wash and dry hands thoroughly before starting to prepare food. Use soap and dry towels.
- Ensure your work area is clean and wiped free of crumbs, liquids and food scraps.
- Clean chopping boards and work surfaces with hot, soapy water after cutting raw meat and between usage for cutting different foods. Raw food such as meats and seafood will transfer harmful bacteria from surfaces to your mouth very easily.
- Thoroughly clean knives and other equipment that have been used for cutting raw meat or fish to prevent cross-contamination. Washing equipment also prevents the transfer of flavours such as those of garlic and onions into your sweet cakes and sauces.
- Egg dishes, meats, seafood and anything that has been cooked must be refrigerated without delay once it has cooled down.
- If meat is frozen, thaw it by leaving it in the fridge overnight or by quickly defrosting it in the microwave. Do not leave it it out on a bench or sink all night.
- Always reheat food thoroughly. Ensure food is brought to boiling point when reheated, not just warmed. Harmful bacteria love warm places and will grow rapidly if the conditions are right.
- Never reheat food more than once.
- If in doubt throw it out. If meat smells pungent or is slimy, bin it. It is not worth the risk. If eggs are past the date on the carton, or milk and other dairy products beyond the 'best before' date, throw them out. Your health is more important.

Feeding your flat
on a budget

As in any household, cooking for one person or cooking for six, it is important to budget your meal spend. There is no point spending masses on your everyday ingredients, and leaving yourselves short for the power, water and all the other expenses we have. Meal time doesn't need to be expensive and you don't need to compromise on nutrition for the price. In fact, with planning and foresight you will save more cash and more calories at the same time.

Plan your meals

Planning allows you to keep your supermarket spending under control. Take 10 minutes each week to sit down and think about what meals can be cooked each day. Use this cookbook to give you the ideas for breakfast, lunch and dinner, and then write a list of ingredients needed. Go to the supermarket or local shops with a list, and you will cut down on impulse buying and overspending. Allow some flexibility – you may see some items on special, but at least you will have covered off every day of the week.

Use the following table to structure your weekly shopping. Take 10 minutes to think creatively about your menu for the week. Use cookbooks or recipe cuttings from magazines for inspiration.

	Monday	Tuesday	Wednesday	Thursday	Friday	Saturday	Sunday
Breakfast							
Snacks							
Lunch							
Snacks							
Dinner							
Dessert							

A weekly shop, instead of every day or every second day, decreases time spent in-store and the chances of making impulse decisions. One shop once a week, with a list, will reduce your food bill.

Shopping on a budget

Decide how much money you have to spend each week on food. Be realistic; don't have a tiny budget and too little food. You don't want to discover, 2–3 days into the week, that takeaways bought with your own cash are the only option.

When you have established a budget, divide the amount you have between each meal – for example I could spend $5 on breakfast and $10 on dinner, or a total of $20 a day for all meals. The challenge then is finding foods in your local store to fit within the budget. If chicken is on special this week, then you could spend more money on the condiments or vegetables to accompany it. The reward for watching your spending on a per meal basis is the enjoyment of having dollars left over for treats or savings at the other end of the week.

Plan your shopping list by breaking it into divisions of where you are going to find these items (an example of this is on the opposite page).

Veges & fruit	Dairy/cold	Frozen
Meat/fish	Cleaning	Personal/pharmacy
Canned food	Deli	Baking/cooking

A list will provide the discipline of buying only what you need and reduce impulse buying. Each week you can try to reduce the amount you are spending, making it into a weekly challenge or game.

Specials and bargains

Take advantage of items on special. If you always shop at the same supermarket, a wide range of items will be available at reduced prices over a period of time. If a product can be stored easily, then it may be a bonus to buy in bulk. Otherwise don't get trapped into buying food items that are not normally consumed.

Some budget shoppers choose to shop at the end of the day, when fresh items have markdown prices. This has limitations of not having the exact cut of meat or vegetable left. The local butcher or greengrocer are still great options for good cuts of meat, plus they give you exactly what you want and the right amount – for example, rather than buying 3 pieces of schnitzel in a pack when you only wanted 2.

It may seem very old-fashioned – but cutting coupons and using reward cards are a great way to save money on purchases. Clip coupons to a noticeboard or place directly into your wallet to use them when out shopping. Add that object to your shopping list, so you remember to use the coupon.

Shop around! Stores compete with each other on prices, and you may as well make the most of this. Providing you are not going too far in your search for the cheapest goods and so wasting time and petrol searching, then bargains can be picked up at competing stores.

Seasonal shopping

Fresh fruit and vegetables are always at the best price when supplied seasonally. Simple oversupply at certain times of the year will drive down prices. While supermarkets may have all vegetables available all year round, they tend to buy out-of-season vegetables from foreign markets, therefore increasing the price significantly because of transport costs. By taking the time to shop at local fruit and vegetable shops or make a trip to the country districts, much cheaper supply of your favourite produce can be found. Moreover, farmers' markets are now more prevalent in local communities, providing a surplus of seasonal vegetables and fruits at very reasonable prices.

Seasonal fruits and vegetables, or even cuts of meat or seafood, can be preserved by freezing or bottling for later use.

Buy local

A good butcher will give you not only the quantity of meat you ask for, but can remove the fat and bones you don't want to pay for. A local fish shop will stock locally caught seafood, and a local fruit shop may supply straight from the grower. You will save money, support your local community and get the freshest quality around.

Freeze ahead

If you have a freezer, use it to store items that are offered at very reasonable prices – sometimes products such as meat are reduced in price substantially for quantity purchases. Buy bulk and then break up into smaller packages and freeze using freezer bags. Remember to label and date all the packages. Food can be thawed the day before or on the day it is to be used if kept in the fridge. Note not to leave goods in the freezer for too long. As a rule, meats shouldn't be frozen for longer than 3 months. Fruit and vegetables will last for up to 6 months.

Leftovers

There is nothing wrong with leftovers. Excess mashed potato can be turned into hash browns for breakfast. Extra cooked rice could become a tuna and rice salad. Too many cooked vegetables can be used in a warm quiche, or any leftover casserole or stew is perfect heated up at the office or school for a hearty lunch.

Take care when reheating that the food is heated through properly. It is best not to reheat cooked rice, as it may contain harmful microbes. Always watch when reheating any meat product that it is hot and not just warmed.

Grow your own
ingredients

Growing your own herbs or vegetables is easy, therapeutic and very rewarding. You don't need a lot of space or too much time caring for small plants and there are ample rewards to your cooking.

Use terracotta, plastic or wooden pots and some good-quality potting mix. Alternatively, find a small patch of an outside garden, turn the soil over with some compost and fertilise regularly for the best results. Keep plants well watered and fed with seaweed or organic blood and bone.

Garden centres can give information about how to grow simple seedlings in your home garden. Either grow from seed and really save yourself some cash or buy seedlings that are ready to be transferred into potting soil.

Vegetables and fruits that can be grown in tubs or small spaces include:
- Asian greens such as bok choy
- Beans and peas
- Capsicums
- Chillies
- Fancy lettuces such as buttercrunch or cos
- Silverbeet and spinach
- Spring onions
- Strawberries
- Some tomato varieties

Great herbs to grow in your garden include:
- Basil
- Chives
- Coriander
- Dill
- Marjoram
- Mint
- Oregano
- Parsley – curly or flat leaf
- Rosemary
- Sage
- Tarragon
- Thyme

If you have a rented property with fruit trees or a ready-built vegetable garden area, take the time to look after it. Remove dead or overripe fruit from the branches of trees or, better still, pick when the fruit has just ripened. If you don't want it – give it away. Any plants or weeds growing in the garden can be removed and used in a compost bin or dug back into a corner of the garden. Plant root vegetables such as carrots and beetroot into well-tilled soil, or corn and potatoes in large areas of land.

Weights and measures

New Zealand Standard metric cup and spoon measures are used in all recipes. All measurements are level.

Easy measuring – Use measuring cups or jugs for liquid measures and sets of 1 cup, ½ cup, ⅓ cup and ¼ cup for dry ingredients.

Brown sugar measurements – Are firmly packed so that the sugar will hold the shape of the cup when tipped out.

Eggs – No. 6 eggs are used as the standard size.

Abbreviations

l = litre
ml = millilitre
cm = centimetre
mm = millimetre
g = gram
kg = kilogram
°C = degrees Celsius

Standard measures

1 cup = 250 millilitres
1 litre = 4 cups
1 tablespoon = 15 millilitres
1 dessertspoon = 10 millilitres
1 teaspoon = 5 millilitres
½ teaspoon = 2.5 millilitres
¼ teaspoon = 1.25 millilitres

Approximate metric/imperial conversions

Weight
25 g = 1 ounce
125 g = 4 ounces
225 g = 8 ounces
500 g = 1 pound
1 kg = 2¼ pounds

Volume
1 litre = 1¾ pints
Measurements
1 cm = ½ inch
20 cm = 8 inches
30 cm = 12 inches

Weights and measures – approximate equivalents

Item	Measure	Weight
breadcrumbs (fresh)	1 cup	50 g
butter	2 tablespoons	30 g
cheese (grated, firmly packed)	1 cup	100 g
cocoa	4 tablespoons	25 g
coconut	1 cup	75 g
cornflour	4 tablespoons	25 g
cream	1/2 pint	300 ml
dried fruit (currants, sultanas, raisins, dates)	1 cup	150–175 g
flour	1 cup	125 g
golden syrup	1 tablespoon	25 g
milk	1 cup	250 ml
oil	1 tablespoon	15 ml
rice, sago	2 tablespoons	25 g
	1 cup	200 g
salt	2 tablespoons	25 g
sugar, white	2 tablespoons	30 g
	1 cup	250 g
sugar, brown	1 cup (firmly packed)	200 g
	1 cup (loosely packed)	125–150 g
sugar, icing	1 cup	150 g
standard No. 6 egg		about 50 g

Before and after equivalent measures

Approximate amounts needed to give measures:
1/3 cup uncooked rice = 1 cup cooked rice
1/3 cup uncooked pasta = 1 cup cooked pasta
2–3 chicken pieces = 1 cup cooked chicken
100 g cheese = 1 cup grated cheese
75 g mushrooms = 1 cup sliced = 1/2 cup cooked
4 toast slices bread = 1 cup fresh breadcrumbs
200 g (two) potatoes = 1 cup mashed potato

Oven know-how

Oven conversions
160°C = 325°F
180°C = 350°F
190°C = 375°F
200°C = 400°F

A guide to oven temperatures and use

Product	°C	°F	Gas No.	Description
meringues, pavlova,	110–140	225–175	¼–1	slow
custards, milk puddings, shortbread, rich fruit cakes casseroles, slow roasting	150–160	300–325	2–3	moderately slow
biscuits, large and small cakes, roasting,	180–190	350–375	4–5	moderate
roasting, sponges, muffins short pastry,	190–220	375–425	5–6	moderately hot
flaky pastry, scones browning toppings	220–230	425–450	6–8	hot
puff pastry	250–260	475–500	9–10	very hot

Oven hints
Cooking temperatures and times given in this book are a guide only as ovens may vary. Always preheat oven to required temperature before food preparation.

Oven racks – position before turning oven on.

Oven positions
  Bottom of oven – use for slow cooking and low temperature cooking
  Middle of oven – for moderate temperature cooking
  Above middle – for quick cooking and high temperature cooking

Fan-forced ovens – refer to the manufacturer's directions as the models vary.

Weights and measures

Breakfast and brunch

We are always told that breakfast is the most important meal of the day. Why? Because it is. We need energy first thing in the morning to feed our minds and bodies and to give us the best possible performance levels. You wouldn't try to start a car without filling up the petrol tank!

By allowing yourself that extra 15–20 minutes in the morning before work, school or daily activities to eat a nutritious and satisfying meal, you will cut out the need for extra snacking throughout the day. It doesn't need to be boring or dull; it can be as simple as some toast, cereal or fruit. Think about what you like eating in the morning and then plan to buy something that can be easily prepared before the morning rush.

New trends towards low-carbohydrate diets might work for weight loss, but it is still important to feed the machine before you begin activity. Carbohydrate meals such as porridge, cereals, muffins or breads provide instant energy. Fruits give you sweetness and flavour as well as important antioxidants and vitamins. Dairy products such as low-fat yoghurts and cheese give your body necessary calcium. With a well-balanced breakfast and other meals you don't need to spend extra money on vitamin and mineral supplements – it all comes from your food.

The weekend brings brunch. Time to rest and sleep and catch up with friends, so your morning meal may be delayed. Instead of using up money at cafés, treat your friends and flatmates to a cooked breakfast at home. It needn't be difficult to piece together a meal, some fresh coffee and a little morning sunshine.

Front: Chocolate and banana porridge, page 19
Back left: Fresh fruit porridge, page 19
Back right: Peach porridge and custard, page 19

Banana caramel pancakes, page 21

Five ways
with porridge oats

Make porridge according to the pack instructions:

Fresh fruit porridge
Serve with fresh raspberries, kiwifruit, strawberries or any seasonal fruit. Drizzle with runny honey.

Chocolate and banana porridge
Add 1 teaspoon of cocoa to the porridge oats. Serve topped with chocolate chips and banana chips.

Jam and cream porridge
While porridge is hot, stir through 3 tablespoons of your favourite jam. Whip cream and place a spoonful on top. Serve immediately.

Peach porridge and custard
In a tall heatproof glass, place spoonfuls of porridge. Heat custard according to instructions. Spoon in warm custard and top with sliced peaches. Repeat layering until glass is full. Finish with custard and slices of peaches.

Scottish porridge
Mix 2 cups of cold porridge with 2 tablespoons whisky and 2 tablespoons brown sugar. Place in glasses and chill. Serve with whipped cream and fresh raspberries.

Yoghurt smoothies

2 bananas
1 cup frozen berries such as
   blueberries, blackberries
   or raspberries

150 ml yoghurt
handful ice cubes

Place all ingredients in a blender or food processor and process until smooth.

SERVES 2

VARIATIONS
- Add 2 scoops ice cream
- Add 2 tablespoons Edmonds Wheat Bran
- Add 2 tablespoons runny honey
- Add 1 teaspoon spirulina powder

Microwave muesli

4 tablespoons oil, such as peanut
   or corn
2 tablespoons honey
1 cup wholegrain oats
1 cup rolled oats or oat flakes

1 cup Edmonds Wheat Bran
½ cup sunflower seeds
½ cup Edmonds Wheat Germ
⅓ cup peanuts, chopped
2–3 tablespoons sesame seeds

Place oil and honey in a very large bowl. Microwave for 30 seconds, just so you can stir the two together. Add all remaining ingredients and mix well. Microwave for 8–9 minutes on High, stirring every 2–3 minutes. Stir well when cooking is completed, and often as muesli cools. It will be a golden colour and become crisp as it cools. When completely cold, store in an airtight container, preferably in the fridge. Serve with milk and fresh fruit.

MAKES 5 CUPS

Banana caramel pancakes

1 cup Champion Self Raising
   Flour, sifted
2 tablespoons caster sugar
1 egg, lightly beaten
⅓ cup sour cream
½ cup milk

25 g butter, melted
extra 50 g butter
⅓ cup brown sugar,
   firmly packed
½ cup cream
2 medium bananas, sliced

Combine flour, sugar, egg, sour cream and milk in a bowl. Beat until smooth. Brush a heated, heavy-based pan with some of the melted butter. Add 2 tablespoons pancake mixture, cook until browned underneath. Turn and brown on other side. Keep warm. Repeat with remaining melted butter and pancake mixture. Combine extra butter, brown sugar and cream in a pan. Stir over heat until sugar is dissolved; bring to boil, remove from heat. Add bananas, stir until heated through. Serve pancakes topped with caramel banana mixture.

SERVES 4

Creamy mushrooms and bacon

4 slices toast bread
   or ciabatta bread
2 tablespoons olive oil
1 onion, finely diced
1 teaspoon sugar
3 bacon rashers, finely chopped
1 clove garlic, crushed

250 g large mushrooms, sliced
1 tablespoon chopped fresh chives
2 tablespoons cream
salt and freshly ground black
   pepper to season
extra chives for garnish

Preheat oven to 190°C. Brush both sides of the slices of bread with olive oil. Place on an oven tray. Cook in oven for about 10 minutes, or until golden brown and crisp. Heat remaining oil in a pan, add onion and sugar; stir over low heat until onion is golden brown. Add bacon and fry until crisp. Add garlic, mushrooms, chives and cream and cook stirring, over medium heat, for about 3 minutes, or until mushrooms are soft. Season to taste. To serve, divide mushroom mixture between warm toast slices, sprinkle with extra chives.

SERVES 4

Courgette and cottage cheese fritters

2 courgettes, grated
2 tablespoons chopped fresh herbs such as parsley or chives
200 g cottage cheese with chives
pinch cayenne pepper
1 egg, beaten
salt and freshly ground black pepper
1 cup Edmonds Standard Grade Flour
1 teaspoon Edmonds Baking Powder
25 g butter

In a medium-sized bowl, mix the courgette and herbs with cottage cheese, cayenne pepper and egg. Season with salt and pepper. Fold in flour and baking powder. Heat a frying pan with butter. Drop spoonfuls into the hot pan and cook on one side until browned. Turn over and cook on the other side, until browned. Drain on absorbent paper before serving with bacon or poached eggs.

SERVES 4

Wheat-free corn fritters

1 cup rice flour
½ cup potato flour
400 g can cream-style corn
2 spring onions, finely chopped
2 eggs, beaten
½ cup grated tasty cheese
¼ cup milk
pinch cayenne pepper
salt and freshly ground black pepper
2 tablespoons oil

In a large bowl sift the rice flour and potato flour. Add the corn, spring onions, eggs, cheese, milk and season well. Mix with a wooden spoon until it makes a soft mixture. Refrigerate for 20 minutes. Heat oil in a frying pan. Drop tablespoonfuls of corn mixture into pan. Cook until golden then turn and cook other side. Drain on absorbent paper. Serve hot.

SERVES 4

Spinach, herb and
feta frittatas (gluten-free)

8 eggs
¾ cup rice flour
4 tablespoons cream
300 g spinach leaves, washed
    and stalks removed

200 g feta cheese, cubed
salt and freshly ground
    black pepper

Preheat oven to 180°C. Break the eggs into a bowl, and beat lightly with a fork or whisk. Mix in rice flour and cream. Spray 12-hole muffin tin or alternatively use paper patty cases. Lay spinach and feta in the tins and pour over the egg mixture. Cook in oven for 15 minutes or until egg is puffed and golden. Season with salt and pepper. Serve with gluten-free toast.

MAKES 12

Tomato and avocado
salsa bruschetta

3 tomatoes
2 avocados
2 tablespoons lemon juice
handful fresh mint leaves
2 tablespoons extra virgin olive oil

salt and freshly ground
    black pepper
1 loaf French bread
100 g gruyere cheese
lemon slices

Preheat oven to 200°C. Remove the core and finely chop tomatoes. Peel avocado, remove stone and dice. Sprinkle over the lemon juice. Roughly chop mint leaves. Add tomato, mint and olive oil to avocado and season well with salt and pepper. Cut the French bread into 4 pieces and cut each piece in half. Lay cheese slices on the top of the bread and grill in hot oven for 2–3 minutes until cheese is bubbling and starting to turn brown. Remove from oven and top each piece with some of the tomato and avocado salsa. Serve immediately with slices of lemon.

SERVES 4

Breakfast and brunch

Buttermilk hotcakes

1¼ cups buttermilk
2 tablespoons butter, melted
1 cup Edmonds Standard Grade Flour
¼ teaspoon salt
¾ teaspoon Edmonds Baking Powder
¾ teaspoon Edmonds Baking Soda
1 egg
extra melted butter to cook

Combine buttermilk and butter in a jug. Sift flour, salt, baking powder and soda into a bowl. Make a well in centre of dry ingredients. Break in egg. Use a wire whisk to mix egg into surrounding flour. Add buttermilk to flour in a steady stream, whisking constantly until mixture is smooth. Heat a heavy-based frying pan or griddle over a medium heat. Brush lightly with butter. Cooking one at a time, pour in enough mixture to make a 10-cm circle. Cook for 3–4 minutes until bubbles appear on the surface. Turn with a spatula and cook for 2–3 minutes. Pile on top of each other to keep warm while cooking remaining hotcakes.

MAKES 8

TOPPING SUGGESTIONS
- Sliced banana and/or hulled, halved strawberries with crème fraîche and drizzled with maple syrup.
- Grilled bacon and drizzled with maple syrup.
- Hulled, halved strawberries and fruit yoghurt.

Spicy baked beans

1 tablespoon olive oil
½ onion, finely sliced
400 g can baked beans
400 g can crushed tomatoes
100 g mushrooms, sliced
1 teaspoon curry powder
½ cup grated cheddar cheese
salt and freshly ground black pepper
2 slices wholemeal bread

Heat the oil in a saucepan. Add the onion and cook for 5 minutes until soft. Add the beans, tomatoes and mushrooms. Cook a further 5 minutes until hot and bubbling. Stir in the curry powder, cheese and season well. Cook until the cheese has melted. Serve the beans on toasted wholemeal bread or baked potatoes.

SERVES 2

How to cook eggs for breakfast or brunch

Some hints and tips to cook your breakfast eggs perfectly.

How to soft- or hard-boil an egg
Place a pot of water on the stove. Always use a small saucepan. Eggs with too much space to roll around and bang into one another are likely to crack. Place the eggs in cold water and then turn on. Don't put cold eggs into hot water as they are likely to crack. Never overboil eggs. Try to always use a timer – it is the easiest way to perfection. If you over boil eggs they will turn black and will be very rubbery. For soft-boiled eggs, where the yolk remains runny, cook for 3–4 minutes. A hard-boiled egg will take 6–7 minutes. You may need to experiment to get it exactly how you like it. Remember: every egg has an air pocket; to stop cracking prick the outside shell with a pin.

How to poach an egg
Use a heavy-based frying pan or very shallow saucepan. If possible, use an enamel, non-stick or aluminium pan to prevent discolouration of the eggs. Fill the pan with water to a depth of about 4 cm, enough to cover an egg when cracked open. Bring the water to a boil, then turn down to simmer. Water that is rapidly boiling will split the white and overcook the egg very quickly. If not confident with cracking an egg directly into the pan, then break each egg into a saucer or cup. Slip the egg into the water so it slides to the side of the pan and the yolk stays in the centre; make sure the water covers the egg so a film forms over the yolk. Cook until the film of white covering the yolk is set and the white is firm. Remove each egg with a fish slice or slotted spoon to allow the water to drain. To test the firmness of the egg yolk, press lightly with a fork, trying not to break it.

Tip: You only need to add ½ teaspoon vinegar or lemon juice to the water if your eggs are not very fresh. This will stop the egg whites from spreading. The fresher the eggs, the better they are for poaching.

Breakfast and brunch

How to fry an egg

Use a heavy-based frying pan, non-stick pan or grill plate. Heat butter or oil or the fat left over after cooking bacon (just enough to stop the egg from sticking). Break each egg into a saucer or cup. Slip onto the hot fat and reduce the heat immediately to stop the egg from toughening. Cook for 3–5 minutes, or until the egg white is firm. Remove each egg with a fish slice. Drain on absorbent paper before serving.

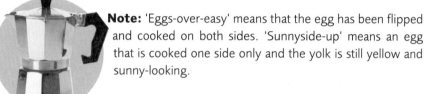

Note: 'Eggs-over-easy' means that the egg has been flipped and cooked on both sides. 'Sunnyside-up' means an egg that is cooked one side only and the yolk is still yellow and sunny-looking.

How to scramble eggs

For one person you need 2 eggs. In a separate jug or bowl beat the eggs with 1 tablespoon cream, milk or yoghurt. Season well with salt and pepper. Heat a heavy-based saucepan, non-stick pan or aluminium frying pan. Melt 2 tablespoons butter in the pan on a low heat; avoid browning the butter. Pour in the egg mixture. Cook, stirring all the time by lifting and turning, keeping it in large soft masses. Remove the egg mixture from the heat just before setting is complete to allow the heat of the pan to finish the cooking. Serve hot on buttered toast.

Tip: The egg will cook quickly – don't take your eyes off it. Make sure the egg mixture does not stay in contact with the bottom of the pan long enough to brown or toughen.
Idea: Any pieces of bacon, chopped chives, cheese, tomatoes, etc can be added to flavour the scrambled eggs.

Tomato and avocado salsa bruschetta, page 23

Front: Tomato, olive and cottage cheese dip, page 29
Centre: Bean and garlic dip, page 30
Back: Sour cream and relish dip, page 29

Snacks and starters

A snack, by definition, is a food eaten between meals to satisfy your hunger. You will be surprised how little food is needed to cure your hunger pangs. Choose small, filling snacks. Protein and vegetables are less guilt-filled than sugar and fatty snacks.

To avoid running to the shop to buy takeaways or fat- or sugar-loaded snacks, try making your own selections. Being prepared with a few good store-cupboard items helps to make nutritious snacks quickly.

Snacks can be turned into starters easily by making them a little more elaborate or simply with a colourful garnish and a small plate. Try flavoured dips with crunchy vegetables or a small plateful of different snacks and starters.

Starters complement the main meal, so choose foods that go with the main but are not the same as it. For example, if serving a dish of meat for the main, it may not be a good idea to have the same meat as the starter. A starter should also be just a small portion of food. It is designed to get the juices flowing and start the appetite before the main event.

Five ways
with egg noodles

Egg noodles are a great snack – try the following to make them into a light hot meal or a more nutritious snack. Cook a 150 g packet of egg noodles to the manufacturer's instructions and add the following to make a difference.

Chicken and mushroom
Heat a small saucepan with 1 teaspoon sesame oil. Add 100 g shredded chicken meat, 100 g sliced mushrooms, 1 finely sliced spring onion and 1 teaspoon soy sauce. Toss through the egg noodles and serve.

Tofu and sweet chilli
Dice 100 g tofu. Sprinkle over 1 teaspoon curry powder. Heat 1 tablespoon oil in a small saucepan and fry the tofu pieces. Add ½ cup corn kernels, 1 finely chopped spring onion and 1 tablespoon sweet chilli sauce. Toss through the egg noodles and serve.

Quick Vietnamese soup
Heat 1 cup liquid beef stock in a medium saucepan until boiling. Slice 1 beef schnitzel into thin strips and drop into the boiling broth. Add 1 diced tomato, 1 diced courgette and 3–4 sliced, button mushrooms. Flavour with fish sauce and sweet chilli sauce. When ready to serve, drop in the egg noodles, stir to mix and serve immediately.

Egg noodle and tuna nest
Finely dice 1 onion, 1 red capsicum and 1 tomato. Mix in a bowl with 2 finely shredded lettuce leaves, a 100 g can flavoured tuna and 2 tablespoons aioli (page 30). Add the egg noodles and toss through. Season to taste. Twirl the noodles around on the end of a fork to form a 'nest'. Place on plate and sprinkle over any extra filling before serving.

Tomato chilli noodles
Heat 1 tablespoon oil in a heavy-based saucepan. Add 2 finely diced tomatoes, 2 tablespoons chopped fresh parsley, ½ onion, finely diced, and 1 tablespoon tomato purée. Stir well and add 1 teaspoon chilli paste. Add egg noodles, toss through and serve with chopped pinenuts or peanuts.

Dips and spreads

Tomato, olive and
cottage cheese dip

½ cup sundried tomatoes
1 clove garlic, crushed
200 g cottage cheese
1 spring onion, sliced thinly

1 tablespoon finely chopped
  black olives
2 tablespoons chopped fresh basil
salt and freshly ground
  black pepper

Chop tomatoes finely. Blend or process garlic, tomatoes and cheese until smooth. Transfer to a bowl and stir in onion, olives and basil. Season to taste with salt and black pepper.

MAKES 2 CUPS

Sour cream and
relish dip

250 g sour cream
½ cup unsweetened yoghurt
3 tablespoons sweet fruit chutney

2–3 tablespoons capers,
  squashed with a fork

Mix all ingredients together in a bowl. Refrigerate before serving.

MAKES 2 CUPS

Peanut dip

1 teaspoon oil
1 small onion, finely chopped
1 cup crunchy peanut butter

¾ cup milk or coconut milk
1 tablespoon chilli sauce
  (optional)

Heat oil in a small saucepan. Cook onion for 5 minutes until soft. Add remaining ingredients to the pan. Stir over a low heat for 4 minutes until mixture is smooth and heated through. Serve warm.

MAKES 2 CUPS

Dips and spreads

Bean and garlic dip

2 x 400 g cans cannellini beans
1 large carrot
1 celery stalk
1 bay leaf or sprig fresh thyme
1 teaspoon salt
1 large red onion, chopped

8 cloves garlic
1/3 cup olive oil
salt and freshly ground black pepper
2 teaspoons chopped chives

Drain the canned beans. Simmer in large, covered saucepan of water with the carrot, celery, bay leaf or thyme for about 30 minutes. Add salt and continue to simmer for another 30 minutes or until the beans have become tender. Remove the vegetables and discard. Drain the beans. Preheat oven to 180°C. Place the onion and garlic on a baking tray and drizzle over the olive oil and season well. Cook in oven until they are tender and lightly browned, for about 20–30 minutes. Mash or process the garlic and onions and the beans to a smooth purée adding a little extra olive oil to help make it creamy. Add the chives. Serve hot or cold.

MAKES 2 CUPS

Aioli

6 cloves garlic
1 teaspoon salt
1 teaspoon Dijon mustard
2 eggs
2 egg yolks

freshly ground black pepper
2 tablespoons white wine vinegar
3 cups soy bean oil or light olive oil
2 tablespoons lemon juice

Preheat oven to 180°C. Roast peeled garlic in oven for 10 minutes until softened, but not too brown. Place salt, mustard, eggs and yolks in food processor or blender. Add garlic and pepper and blend briefly. Scrape down bowl. Add vinegar and blend again. With the motor on, slowly add oil through feed tube. Continue until smooth and thick, finally adding the lemon juice. Serve cold.

MAKES 3–4 CUPS

Quick nachos

200 g corn chips
400 g can refried beans or mild chilli beans
1 cup grated tasty cheese
1 avocado, sliced, to serve
250 g sour cream, to serve

Preheat oven to 200°C. Put corn chips into a large ovenproof serving dish. Top corn chips with hot refried beans and sprinkle with cheese. Bake in oven for 8 minutes or until all the cheese has melted. Serve with avocado slices and spoon over sour cream.

SERVES 4-6

Pita bread pizzas

4 pita breads
2 tablespoons olive oil
4 tablespoons tomato relish
4 slices ham, thinly sliced
350 g can pineapple pieces, drained
1 tomato, diced
8 anchovies (optional)
1 cup grated mozzarella cheese

Preheat oven to 220°C. Place the pita breads on a baking tray. Brush with oil. Spread the relish evenly over the tops of breads. Top with shredded ham, pineapple pieces, tomato and anchovies, if using. Sprinkle with mozzarella cheese. Bake in oven for 8 minutes or until cheese has melted and is starting to bubble. Serve immediately, whole or cut into triangles.

SERVES 4

Snacks and starters

Rustic caramelised onion and tomato tarts

3 tablespoons olive oil
4 red onions, thinly sliced
2 tablespoons brown sugar
2 tablespoons balsamic vinegar
400 g Edmonds Flaky Puff Pastry
24 cherry tomatoes, halved
salt and freshly ground black pepper
⅓ cup finely grated parmesan cheese to sprinkle

Heat oil in a heavy-based frying pan. Cook onions over a very low heat for 20 minutes, stirring regularly. Stir in brown sugar and vinegar and cook for a further 2 minutes. Cool. Preheat oven to 200°C. Roll pastry out into a 32-cm x 24-cm rectangle. Cut into 4 equal-sized rectangles. Line a baking tray with baking paper. Transfer pastry rectangles to the tray. Refrigerate for 15 minutes. Divide caramelised onion between the pastry, spreading evenly and leaving a 3-cm border. Arrange tomatoes cut-size up on top of onion. Season and sprinkle with parmesan. Bake in oven for 20 minutes or until the pastry border is risen and golden.

SERVES 4

Italian sandwiches

1 loaf French bread
100 g basil pesto
100 g salami slices
150 g baby spinach leaves
200 g mozzarella cheese slices
2 large tomatoes, sliced thinly
salt and freshly ground black pepper
greaseproof paper
string

Cut bread stick lengthways through the middle. Spread both inner sides liberally with pesto. Lay salami slices on one side of the bread, top with spinach leaves, cheese slices and tomato slices. Place the top of bread on top of the other side. Carefully wrap the whole bread stick with greaseproof paper. Tie string tightly around the bread stick at 10-cm intervals. Using a serrated knife cut between the pieces of string. Refrigerate the sandwiches before serving. The sandwiches are perfect to be made the day before a picnic or event.

SERVES 6

Calzone

DOUGH
1½ teaspoons sugar
1¼ cups warm water
2 tablespoons Edmonds Active Yeast
3 cups Champion High Grade Flour
1½ teaspoons salt
¼ cup olive oil

FILLING
2 tablespoons basil pesto
1½ cups grated mozzarella cheese
2 large tomatoes, sliced
1 red capsicum, sliced
40 g salami, thinly sliced
freshly ground black pepper
rock salt or grated parmesan cheese to sprinkle

Dissolve sugar in the warm water. Sprinkle yeast over water and set aside in a warm place for 10 minutes until frothy. Combine flour and salt in a large bowl. Stir in frothy yeast mixture and oil. Mix to a soft dough. Transfer dough to a liberally floured surface and knead for 5 minutes until smooth and elastic. Place the dough in an oiled bowl. Turn dough to coat with oil. Cover with plastic wrap and stand in a warm place for 45 minutes until dough is well risen.

Preheat oven to 220°C. Divide dough in half. Roll each portion into a 25-cm-diameter circle. Place one circle on a lightly greased baking tray. Spread with pesto to within 1 cm of the dough edge. Sprinkle mozzarella cheese over the pesto, then top with tomato, red capsicum and salami. Season with pepper.

Brush edge of dough with a little oil. Position the remaining circle of dough on top and seal edges with your fingertips. Brush top lightly with a little olive oil. Sprinkle with rock salt or parmesan cheese. Bake in oven for 10 minutes, then reduce temperature to 200°C and bake for a further 15–20 minutes until golden. Serve hot, cut into wedges.

SERVES 6

Snacks and starters

Tostadas

8 x 20-cm diameter flour tortillas
450 g can refried beans
3 tablespoons bottled tomato salsa
2 small avocados, sliced
2 cups shredded lettuce
2 cups sliced cooked chicken meat
16 cherry tomatoes, halved
250 g sour cream, to serve

DRESSING
2 tablespoons lemon or lime juice
¼ teaspoon salt
½ teaspoon ground cumin
¼ cup oil

Warm tortillas according to instructions on the packet. Heat refried beans and tomato salsa in a saucepan. Spread each tortilla with bean mixture. Top with avocado slices, lettuce, chicken and tomatoes. Serve with sour cream. Sprinkle with dressing. To make the dressing, combine all ingredients in a small bowl or jar. Mix well.

SERVES 4

Bacon and egg pie

2 sheets Edmonds Flaky Puff Pastry
1 onion, diced
1 cup chopped bacon

½ cup mixed vegetables
2 tablespoons spicy chutney
6 eggs
milk

Preheat oven to 200°C. Use 1 sheet of pastry to line a 20-cm square shallow cake tin. Sprinkle onion, bacon and mixed vegetables evenly over pastry. Dot the chutney on top. Break eggs evenly over, piercing the yolks so they run slightly. Carefully lift second sheet of pastry over filling. Brush top with milk. Bake in oven for 40 minutes or until well risen and golden. To serve cut into squares. Serve hot or cold.

SERVES 4

Italian sandwiches, page 32

Winter roasted vegetable salad, page 39

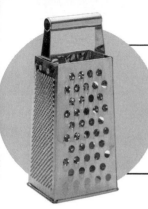

How to choose a healthy snack

When hunger kicks in, there is no need to go for the junk food. Sugary or fatty foods may gratify your hunger for five minutes, but will pick your energy levels up then drop you down just as quick. There are easy ways to reduce your inclination to reach for the wrong kind of snacks.

- Never shop hungry – Always do your weekly shop after having breakfast or lunch. This will reduce the temptation to put bad snack foods in your trolley. Have a list and shop for what is on your list. Treats are OK, but only every now and then, not every day!

- Have healthy goodies in the fridge – Choose baby carrots, cottage cheese, yoghurts, tasty cheeses, rice snacks, fruits and other vegetables instead of cakes and sweets. Think about what your favourite fresh foods are, such as fresh berries, and have them on hand. Take a box of cereal to work or your study area to kill the extreme hunger times.

- Anticipate your hunger – There are times in the day when we all feel hungry. Sometimes we mistake tiredness for hunger and usually an afternoon slump is easily appeased by a snack. Anticipate this with a bowl of fruit in your house or work/study area. Carry a bag of nuts or raisins, or even a packet of instant soup, or extra sandwich around with you to have an instant snack, instead of spending money at the fast-food counter or vending machine.

- Replenish your fruit bowl – Fruit has vitamins and minerals that we need and can give the sugar satisfaction that we crave. Keep your fruit bowl well stocked with yummy fruits you enjoy eating.

- Drive past the takeaways outlets – Think about how marvellous you will feel bypassing the takeaway shops. Save money *and* negative calories.

Salads

A salad can be made really interesting by adding new, unusual and tasty ingredients to the salad staples or even by making an interesting dressing. When buying fresh salad ingredients, store them well (a vegetable crisper is ideal) to get the most out of them when it comes time to prepare.

When preparing salads, make sure that all the vegetables are washed properly and drained of extra water. Since fresh, uncooked ingredients hide little, there is nothing worse than biting down on a piece of grit or a little crawling insect or caterpillar. Tear salad leaves up into bite-sized pieces as cutting with a knife will bruise the leaves and turn them brown quickly.

All pieces in a salad should be bite-sized. Rule of thumb is that a salad should be able to be eaten with just a fork. Many vegetables can be sliced a day in advance and then assembled just before serving. Having a selection of vegetable bites in the fridge also helps if you need a healthy snack. To retain moisture, store prepared vegetables in the fridge either in a bowl of water or wrapped up in damp kitchen towels or plastic bags.

When it's time to assemble a salad, use a large bowl and mix all the ingredients together, leaving out any of the less manageable ingredients such as feta cheese or tuna. Toss the ingredients in the desired dressing. Arrange the lettuce leaves and other vegetables on a platter or salad bowl and top with final ingredients.

A salad can be a meal in a bowl. Don't be scared to experiment with different vegetables or other delicate ingredients to get a great flavour explosion.

Five easy
salad dressings

Basic vinaigrette
½ cup extra virgin olive oil
1½ tablespoons white wine vinegar
¼ teaspoon Dijon mustard
1 clove garlic, crushed
salt and freshly ground black pepper
1 tablespoon chopped fresh herbs (optional)

Combine ingredients in a bowl and whisk until combined, or place ingredients in a jar and shake well.

Honey and mustard
Add to basic vinaigrette:
1 tablespoon honey
1 tablespoon wholegrain mustard

Soy and sesame
Add to basic vinaigrette:
½ teaspoon sesame oil
1 tablespoon soy sauce
1 teaspoon toasted sesame seeds

Lime and chilli
Omit the vinegar and Dijon mustard from basic vinaigrette then add:
½ teaspoon finely grated lime rind
1 tablespoon lime juice
1 tablespoon sweet chilli sauce

Note: Extra virgin olive oil will become cloudy and thicken when it is refrigerated. It will liquefy again at room temperature. You can use lemon juice, lime juice, or flavoured red or white wine vinegar in place of the vinegar. If you prefer a sharper dressing, reduce the oil by 1 tablespoon. Use only enough vinaigrette to coat the salad leaves.

Caesar salad dressing

1 egg
1 anchovy, drained and roughly chopped
2 teaspoons white vinegar
1 teaspoon lemon juice
1 clove garlic, crushed
¼ cup olive oil
freshly ground black pepper

Cook the egg in boiling water for 1 minute. Drain. Break open egg and tip into small bowl. Add anchovy, vinegar, lemon juice and garlic. Whisk vigorously to combine. Add oil in a continuous stream, whisking constantly. Season to taste with pepper.

Winter roasted
vegetable salad

4 carrots, peeled
3 parsnips, peeled
½ pumpkin, peeled and seeds removed
2 medium kumara, peeled
6 cloves garlic, sliced thinly
1 red capsicum, seeds removed
1 red onion, sliced thinly
¼ cup extra virgin olive oil
salt and freshly ground black pepper
Aioli (page 30)

Preheat oven to 200°C. Cut carrots and parsnips into 5-cm sticks. Peel and dice pumpkin and kumara. Line a roasting dish with baking paper. Place all vegetables in the roasting dish. Spread out and sprinkle over olive oil, salt, pepper and garlic. Cook in oven for 40 minutes. In another roasting dish lay the capsicum and red onion rings. Cook in oven for 20 minutes or until capsicum just starts to brown. Remove from oven and allow vegetables to cool slightly. Lay all the vegetables on a salad platter as a side accompaniment to a meat dish or on its own as a vegetarian supper. Serve with Aioli.

SERVES 4

Tip: When roasting vegetables, keep the size of all the vegetables the same so they cook evenly and are ready at the same time.

Salads

Pumpkin orzo salad

250 g orzo or risoni pasta
½ butternut squash or pumpkin, peeled and seeds removed
4 cloves garlic, crushed
¼ cup olive oil
salt and freshly ground black pepper

200 g feta cheese
4 tablespoons chopped fresh parsley
4 tablespoons chopped fresh chives
¼ cup extra virgin olive oil

Preheat oven to 180°C. Cook pasta in boiling salted water for 10 minutes. Drain well, rinse in hot water and allow to cool. Dice the pumpkin into small 2-cm pieces. Place pumpkin and garlic pieces on a baking tray, drizzle with olive oil and season with salt and pepper. Cook in oven for 30 minutes, until pumpkin pieces are tender. Remove from oven and allow to cool. In a large bowl or serving platter, place the cooked pasta and pumpkin. Cut feta cheese into small cubes. Sprinkle cheese and herbs over the top of pasta and pumpkin. Season well to taste and sprinkle with extra virgin olive oil.

SERVES 4-6

Silverbeet, orange and haloumi salad

8 silverbeet leaves
4 oranges
180 g haloumi cheese
4 tablespoons olive oil or rice bran oil
2 slices bread, cut into 1-cm cubes
2-3 spring onions, thinly sliced
150 g crispy noodles

VINAIGRETTE
⅓ cup olive oil
½ cup red wine vinegar
1 teaspoon wholegrain mustard
salt and freshly ground black pepper

Wash the silverbeet leaves. Cut away the white centre stalk from each leaf. Shred the leaves very finely. Peel the oranges and cut into small chunks. Cut the haloumi into thin strips. Heat oil in a heavy-based frying pan. Add the haloumi strips and bread cubes and brown on each side for about 1-2 minutes. Drain on absorbent paper. Place all the salad ingredients in a large bowl or serving platter and toss well. Put all the vinaigrette ingredients in a glass jar with a lid. Shake well. Before serving, pour the vinaigrette over the salad ingredients and toss well.

SERVES 4

Chickpea and beetroot salad

4 medium beetroot
¼ cup olive oil
¼ cup brown sugar
2 x 400 g cans chickpeas, drained
4 spring onions, sliced thinly
4 tablespoons chopped fresh parsley, plus extra for garnish
2 stalks celery, thinly sliced

YOGHURT DRESSING
1 cup natural unsweetened yoghurt
1 tablespoon lemon juice
¼ teaspoon dry mustard
salt and freshly ground black pepper

Preheat oven to 180°C. Wash the beetroot. Place in a large saucepan, cover with water and bring to the boil. Cook for 5 minutes. Drain and run under cold water. Peel the beetroot with vegetable peeler or knife, the skin should come away easily. Cut beetroot into thin wedges. Place on a baking tray and drizzle over olive oil and brown sugar. Cook in oven for 30 minutes, or until softened. Remove from oven and allow to cool.

In a large bowl or serving platter place the beetroot wedges, chickpeas, spring onions, parsley and celery. To make the dressing, stir all ingredients until combined. (Makes 1 cup.) Chill before using. To serve, mix in the yoghurt dressing and sprinkle with extra chopped parsley.

SERVES 4

Chicken and apricot salad

8 boneless chicken thighs, skin on
salt and freshly ground
    black pepper
300 g green beans
400 g can apricots, cut into pieces
6 lettuce leaves
2 tablespoons chopped chives
    or parsley
100 g snow pea sprouts

DRESSING
½ cup olive oil
¼ cup cider or white wine
    vinegar
½ cup plain non-fat yoghurt
¼ cup chopped fresh basil
    or parsley
1 tablespoon lemon juice

Preheat oven to 200°C. Season thigh fillets with salt and pepper. Place the chicken on a baking tray lined with foil. Cook at top of oven for 20 minutes, or until the chicken is golden and juices run clear. Remove chicken, cover and set aside. Cut the warm chicken into chunky pieces. Leave skin on or off as wished. Cut tops and tails off the green beans and cut in half. Blanch in some boiling water for 5 minutes. Toss the chicken, apricots, beans, lettuce, herbs and snow pea sprouts together in a large bowl or serving platter. Shake the dressing ingredients together in a jar or mix in a small bowl. Pour over the salad and serve immediately.

SERVES 4

Silverbeet, orange and haloumi salad, page 40

Easy seafood chowder, page 48

Vietnamese noodle salad

200 g vermicelli rice noodles
4 tablespoons lime or lemon juice
3 tablespoons sugar
salt and freshly ground
    black pepper
1 red onion, halved
    and finely sliced
250 g savoy cabbage,
    finely shredded
1 large carrot, grated

2 cooked boneless chicken
    breasts, skin removed
2 tablespoons vegetable oil
3 tablespoons chopped fresh
    mint leaves
2 tablespoons chopped fresh
    coriander leaves
1 tablespoon roasted peanuts,
    roughly chopped

Soak the rice noodles in boiling water for 10 minutes, until softened. Drain well and set aside. Mix the juice, sugar, salt and pepper in a bowl. Add the onion and leave to marinate for 30 minutes. In a large, shallow serving bowl, toss the cabbage, carrot and noodles together. Cut the chicken into strips, and add to the salad with the onion, marinade and oil. Toss well to mix. Just before serving, fold in the mint and coriander and scatter over the peanuts.

SERVES 4–6

Tabbouleh

1 cup burghul (cracked wheat)
2 tablespoons chopped fresh mint
1 cup chopped fresh parsley
2 tomatoes, chopped

2 tablespoons oil
¼ cup lemon juice
salt and freshly ground
    black pepper

Put burghul in a bowl. Cover with boiling water. Leave to stand for 30 minutes. Stir and drain if necessary. Add the mint, parsley, tomatoes, oil and lemon juice. Stir to combine. Season to taste with salt and pepper. Chill before serving.

SERVES 6

Salads

Gado gado

- 250 g new potatoes, cut into bite-sized pieces
- 3 carrots, peeled
- 250 g green beans, halved
- 250 g cabbage, core removed and thinly shredded
- 1 small cucumber, sliced
- 200 g bean sprouts
- 4 hard-boiled eggs, quartered
- ½ cup roasted peanuts, roughly chopped

DRESSING
- 1 tablespoon vegetable oil
- 1 small onion, finely diced
- 2 cloves garlic, crushed
- 1 red chilli, finely chopped
- 1 cup crunchy peanut butter
- 1 cup coconut milk
- ½ cup water
- 1 tablespoon soy sauce
- 1 tablespoon tomato sauce

Cook the potatoes in lightly salted water until just tender. Drain and leave until cool enough to handle. Cut the carrots into thin strips and then put into a pan of boiling salted water and blanch for 5 minutes. Drain, refresh in cold water then drain again thoroughly. Repeat with the beans and cabbage, allowing 3–5 minutes blanching time for the beans, 3 minutes for the cabbage.

To make the dressing, heat the oil in a heavy-based pan. Add the onion, garlic and chilli and cook gently for 5 minutes. Add the peanut butter, coconut milk and water. Bring to the boil, stirring constantly. Lower the heat and add the soy sauce and tomato sauce. Remove from the heat, stir well and leave to cool.

Arrange all of the vegetables and the hard-boiled eggs on a large serving platter. Scatter over the roasted peanuts. To serve, spoon some of the dressing over the eggs and vegetables. Serve the remaining dressing separately.

SERVES 4–6

Grilled chicken caesar salad

2 single boneless chicken breasts, skin removed
¼ cup olive oil
2 tablespoons lemon juice
freshly ground black pepper
2 cups stale bread cubes (French bread or toast-sliced bread is ideal)
1 cos lettuce
12 anchovy fillets
shavings of parmesan cheese
Caesar salad dressing (page 38)

Place chicken breasts between 2 sheets of plastic wrap. Beat lightly with a heavy object (e.g. a rolling pin) to flatten to an even thickness of about 1 cm. Place in a single layer in a shallow dish. Combine 2 tablespoons of the oil, the lemon juice and pepper. Pour over chicken, turning to coat. Cover and refrigerate for 2–4 hours. Cook chicken under a preheated grill or on a barbecue for 4–5 minutes on each side until cooked through. Set aside to cool.

To make the croutons, pour remaining oil into a heated frying pan. Add bread cubes and cook until golden, turning frequently. Wash and dry lettuce leaves. Slice chicken into strips. Combine lettuce, chicken, anchovy fillets and Parmesan cheese in a large bowl or serving platter. Pour over dressing. Toss to combine. Scatter over croutons.

SERVES 4–6

Salads

Soups

The best way to get a flavourful soup is to use good ingredients. While it is easy to throw all the old vegetables in the fridge into a large pot, boil and then blend, the flavour will be lost from old and tired vegetables. Fresh leafy vegetables such as spinach and silverbeet are best when the leaves are crisp.

Get extra flavour from your soups by adding strips of bacon or bacon hocks. Beef bones or chicken bones can be added if you don't have time to make your own stock, but just remember to remove all the bones before blending. Ham hocks bring a real depth of flavour to your soup. After cooking, remove the hocks or bones and cut away the skin. Remove the meat, slice up and return to your soup for a chunky, meaty flavour.

Know your soups

 A **bisque** is a rich and creamy soup, usually made from seafood. It has a velvety texture and is made from slow-cooking shells and bones.

 A **broth** is more like a stock. It is made by simmering meat, fish or poultry with vegetables in water. Broth can be a light soup or added to other ingredients to make a more hearty soup.

 A **chowder** is chunky, hearty and contains fish, vegetables or chicken. Shellfish chowders are well known because of the salty sea flavour that mixes well with potatoes.

 A **consommé** is a French term for a very clear soup made by reducing stock and then sieving. A stock is the rich liquid that is made by simmering poultry, meat or fish bones in water. Vegetables are added to give flavour, but then discarded and strained to leave just the liquid.

 A **gumbo** is native to America, typically from New Orleans. It is traditionally served over rice and contains a variety of meat and vegetables.

Minestrone

1 tablespoon olive oil
1 onion, diced
2 cloves garlic, crushed
2 rashers rindless bacon, chopped
1 stalk celery, sliced
1 medium potato, peeled and diced
2 carrots, peeled and diced
2 x 400 g cans tomatoes in juice, chopped
1 tablespoon tomato paste
3 cups liquid chicken or vegetable stock
½ cup macaroni
300 g can butter beans, drained and rinsed
½ cup sliced green beans
½ cup frozen peas
salt and freshly ground black pepper

Heat oil in a large saucepan. Cook onion, garlic and bacon for 5 minutes until onion is soft. Add celery, potato, carrot, tomatoes, tomato paste, stock and macaroni. Bring to the boil. Reduce heat and simmer for 30 minutes. Add beans and peas and simmer for a further 10 minutes. Season to taste. Ladle hot soup into warm bowls.

SERVES 4-6

Easy seafood chowder

25 g butter
½ medium onion, diced
1 large potato, peeled and diced
3 tablespoons Champion Standard Grade Flour
3 cups liquid fish stock
1 cup water
100 g white fish fillets
6-8 scallops or mussels
200 g cocktail shrimps with juice
½ cup cream
½ teaspoon curry powder
1 tablespoon chopped fresh parsley

In a large saucepan melt the butter, and cook the onion and potato. Stir in the flour and cook until frothy. Gradually add the fish stock and water, stirring all the time. Bring to the boil and then cook for 10-15 minutes, until the potato is tender. Dice the fish fillets and scallops or mussels. Add to the pan with the shrimps and cook for 2 minutes. Stir in the cream, curry powder and parsley. Cook for a further 5 minutes. Serve immediately while hot.

SERVES 6

Spicy lentil and carrot soup, page 50

Pea and bacon risotto, page 54

Creamy corn chowder

1 large onion, finely diced
2 tablespoons olive oil
3 large potatoes, peeled and
   diced to 1-cm cubes
2 celery stalks, finely diced
1 red capsicum, seeds removed
   and finely diced
1 cup liquid vegetable or chicken
   stock
2 cups milk
450 g can corn kernels
450 g can cream-style corn
3 spring onions, finely sliced
salt and freshly ground
   black pepper
3 tablespoons finely chopped
   coriander or parsley
2 tablespoons cream

In a large saucepan, cook onion in oil until softened but not coloured. Add the potatoes and cook for 10 minutes. Add the remaining ingredients, except coriander and seasonings. Bring to the boil then simmer until potatoes are cooked through. Purée half of the mixture in a blender or food processor, leaving half the mixture chunky. Adjust seasoning with salt and pepper to taste and gently reheat. Stir through freshly chopped herbs and cream just before serving.

SERVES 4-6

Pea and ham soup

1 cup split peas
1 teaspoon Edmonds Baking Soda
3 cups boiling water
1 onion, diced
1 ham or bacon hock
4 cups water
3-4 tablespoons bacon stock
   powder
freshly ground black pepper

Put the dried peas into a bowl with the baking soda. Pour boiling water onto peas, cool, then leave to soak overnight in refrigerator. Next day, drain peas. Put the peas, onion and hock into a large saucepan. Add water and bacon stock powder. Bring to the boil, cover and leave to simmer about 45 minutes. Remove the ham hock. Purée the soup mixture and return to the saucepan. Remove the meat from the bone of the ham hock. remove any skin or gristle and chop meat finely. Add to the saucepan. Check the seasoning, it may be necessary to add only pepper. Heat through and serve.

SERVES 4-6

Soups

Mussel chowder

100 g streaky bacon, diced
1 large onion, diced
1 stalk celery, chopped
1 green capsicum, seeds removed and diced
2 medium potatoes, peeled and diced
1 bay leaf
2 cups water
salt and freshly ground black pepper
5 tablespoons Champion Standard Grade Flour
3 cups milk
400 g cooked shelled mussels, chopped
2 tablespoons chopped fresh parsley

Gently fry the bacon in a saucepan, until it starts to brown. Add onion and celery and cook until golden. Add capsicum, potatoes, bay leaf and water, and season to taste. Bring to the boil and simmer until potatoes are tender. Mix flour with ½ cup of the milk and stir into the chowder. Stir until boiling. Add the rest of the milk and the mussels and simmer for 4–5 minutes. Serve garnished with chopped parsley.

SERVES 4–6

Spicy lentil and carrot soup

1 cup red lentils
2 cups boiling water
2–3 tablespoons olive oil
1 red onion, thinly sliced
8 cherry tomatoes, halved
6 carrots, peeled
1 tablespoon curry powder
¼ cup coconut cream or yoghurt
4–8 fresh coriander leaves, mint or parsley

Cook the lentils in the water for 10–12 minutes or until tender. Strain well. Heat the oil in a pan and cook the onion for about 5 minutes until starting to brown. Add the tomatoes and heat through. Cook the carrots in boiling salted water for 15 minutes. Drain and mash. Mix together the carrot, curry powder and cooked lentils and Spoon into 4 bowls. Top each with the onion, tomatoes, a dollop of coconut cream or yoghurt and a few fresh coriander, mint or parsley leaves.

SERVES 4

Creamy tomato
and basil soup

1 tablespoon olive oil
1 onion, finely diced
1 clove garlic, crushed
2 x 400 g cans tomatoes in juice, chopped
1 tablespoon sugar
1½ cups liquid chicken or vegetable stock

½ cup cream
2 tablespoons shredded basil leaves
salt and freshly ground black pepper
basil leaves, to garnish

Heat oil in a large, heavy-based saucepan. Cook onion for 4–5 minutes until soft. Add garlic, tomatoes, sugar and stock. Bring to the boil. Reduce heat and simmer for 20 minutes. Purée in batches in a food processor. Return to saucepan. Add cream and basil. Heat gently – do not allow to boil. Season to taste. Ladle into warm bowls. Garnish with basil. Serve with croutons.

SERVES 4

Mushroom Soup

50 g butter
1 onion, diced
500 g mushrooms, sliced
3 tablespoons Champion Standard Grade Flour
2 cups milk

1 cup liquid chicken stock
½ teaspoon salt
white pepper
1 teaspoon lemon juice
chopped parsley or chives

Melt butter in a saucepan. Add onion and mushrooms. Cook until onion is clear. Stir in the flour. Cook, stirring, for 1 minute. Gradually add milk and stock, stirring constantly. Bring to the boil. Cook for 5 minutes or until soup thickens slightly. Add salt, pepper and lemon juice. Serve garnished with parsley or chives.

SERVES 4

Note: For extra flavour sprinkle with chopped crispy bacon rashers.

Soups

French onion soup

50 g butter
6 medium onions, thinly sliced
1 teaspoon sugar
4 cups liquid beef stock
salt and freshly ground
black pepper
¼ cup dry sherry
4–6 slices cheese on toast

Melt butter in a saucepan. Add onions and sugar. Cook slowly for 20 minutes or until onions are golden. Add beef stock. Bring to the boil then cover and simmer for 15 minutes. Season with salt and pepper to taste. Just before serving add sherry. Grill cheese on toast. Cut into triangles or squares and place on soup.

SERVES 4

Leek and potato soup

5 medium potatoes, peeled and chopped
2 teaspoons oil or butter
2 small leeks, thinly sliced
1 clove garlic, crushed
200 g bacon pieces, finely chopped
6 cups liquid chicken stock
1 bay leaf
2 sprigs parsley
1 cup milk
¼ cup chopped fresh parsley
salt and freshly ground
black pepper

Cook potatoes in boiling water until tender, drain and mash. Set aside. Heat oil in a large saucepan. Add leeks, garlic and bacon. Cook without browning until leeks are tender. Pour in stock. Add bay leaf and parsley sprigs. Bring to the boil. Reduce heat and simmer for 20 minutes. Remove bay leaf and parsley sprigs. Add mashed potato. Simmer for 15 minutes. Stir in milk and parsley. Season to taste with salt and pepper. Ladle into warm bowls. Garnish with a sprinkle of pepper.

SERVES 6

Quick pasta and rice

Pasta and rice are the perfect foods for cheap meals. They are cost-effective, nutritious and can be matched to many foods.

For pasta, allow between 75 g and 125 g of dried pasta, or about 90 g of fresh pasta, per person. If you've cooked too much pasta, don't worry – leftover pasta is perfect to reheat the next day. Toss the pasta with a small amount of oil and store in a sealed plastic container. Microwaving is the best way to reheat pasta, making sure that the container you reheat it in is microwave-proof. Alternatively, place pasta in a colander and hold under hot running water until warm and then toss with hot sauce.

Leftover pasta can be layered in a gratin dish with vegetables and tomato pasta sauce and topped with parmesan cheese and then baked. Or, use as an omelette or frittata filling or toss with salad dressing and crisp vegetables for a quick salad and interesting lunch.

However, it is best not to reheat rice. Allow about ½ cup dried rice per person and cook only what you need. Cold rice can be used for salads and other dishes, but reheated rice may contain dangerous microbes. See 'How to cook perfect white rice' (page 60) for the perfect rice texture.

Pea and **bacon risotto**

6 cups liquid chicken stock
25 g butter
6 bacon rashers, chopped coarsely
2 cloves garlic, crushed
1 medium onion, finely diced
2 cups arborio rice
¾ cup dry white wine (optional)

1½ cups frozen peas
½ cup finely grated
  parmesan cheese
2 tablespoons coarsely chopped
  fresh chives
salt and freshly ground
  black pepper

Heat stock in a medium saucepan. Bring to a simmer. Meanwhile, melt butter in a large saucepan. Cook bacon, garlic and onion, stirring, until onion is soft. Add rice and stir to coat in butter mixture. Stir in wine and simmer, uncovered, until the liquid is absorbed. Stir in ½ cup of the hot stock and cook, stirring over a low heat, until the liquid is absorbed. Continue adding stock mixture, a cupful at a time, stirring until absorbed between each addition. Total cooking time should be about 25 minutes or until rice is tender. Place the peas in a heatproof bowl and cover with boiling water, stand for 5 minutes, then drain. Gently stir the peas, parmesan and chives into the risotto. Season to taste with salt and pepper. Serve topped with extra parmesan cheese and extra chopped chives, if desired.

SERVES 4

Easy ham and mozzarella cannelloni, page 56

Nasi goreng, page 57

One pot savoury
beans and rice

1 tablespoon vegetable oil
1 onion, sliced
2 teaspoons curry powder
1 teaspoon turmeric
2 cloves garlic, crushed
1½ cups long-grain rice, washed

400 g can tomatoes in juice, chopped
½ cup water
2 cups sliced courgettes
1 cup sliced green beans
400 g can red kidney beans

Heat oil in a frying pan. Cook onion, curry powder and turmeric for 3–4 minutes, stirring frequently. Add garlic and cook for a further minute. Stir in rice, tomatoes in juice and water. Reduce heat and simmer, uncovered, for 15–18 minutes until rice is cooked. Stir regularly to prevent rice from sticking to the pan. All liquid should be absorbed at this stage. Stir in vegetables and beans and cook over heat for 4–5 minutes until vegetables are tender. Transfer to a serving dish. Serve immediately.

SERVES 4

Fettuccine with
bacon, mushrooms and blue cheese

½ teaspoon salt
500 g fettuccine or other 'long' pasta
2 tablespoons olive oil
1 onion, finely sliced
3 cloves garlic, crushed

6 rashers bacon, diced
200 g button mushrooms, sliced
⅓ cup cream
150 g blue cheese
salt and freshly ground black pepper

Heat a large saucepan of water and add salt when it begins to boil. Add the pasta and cook for 10–12 minutes until tender to the bite. Drain, reserving 1 cup of the salted pasta water, and set aside.

In a large frying pan, heat the oil. Add the onion and garlic and sauté until onion is clear. Add the bacon and fry until crispy. Add the mushrooms. When mushrooms are soft, pour in the cream and boil, stirring all the time. Return the pasta to the pan and add 1 cup of the reserved pasta liquid to blend. Crumble in the blue cheese and season to taste. Serve immediately with crusty bread.

SERVES 4

Spinach and salami
with penne

1 tablespoon butter
1 onion, diced
1 clove garlic, crushed
200 g salami, sliced into thin pieces

2–3 bunches spinach, washed and chopped
250 g penne or other 'short' pasta

Melt butter in a large frying pan. Add onion, garlic and salami. Cook until onion is clear and salami begins to crispen. Stir in spinach and cook for a further 2 minutes or until spinach is dark green, stirring constantly. Serve over hot pasta.

SERVES 4

Ham and mozzarella cannelloni

1 tablespoon butter, for greasing
500 ml ready-made pasta sauce
1 x packet fresh lasagne sheets
8 slices ham

200 g grated mozzarella cheese
salt and freshly grated black pepper
50 g parmesan cheese, grated

Preheat oven to 180°C. Grease a 22-cm loaf tin or baking dish with butter. Spoon in half the ready-made pasta sauce. Lay out the lasagne sheets, place ham slices on top and then three-quarters of the mozzarella. Sprinkle with salt and pepper to taste. Roll the sheets up encasing the ham and cheese. Cut to fit the loaf tin. Lay the rolls in dish and pile up on top of each other filling the tin. Pour over the remaining pasta sauce. Place extra grated mozzarella on top and sprinkle with parmesan cheese. Bake in oven for 40–50 minutes or until pasta is cooked. Serve with a fresh green salad.

SERVES 4

Nasi goreng
(Indonesian fried rice)

750 g long-grain rice
7 tablespoons peanut oil
375 g stir-fry beef
3 eggs
1 teaspoon dried sambal oelek
  or crushed chilli
½ teaspoon salt
2 onions, diced
4 cloves garlic, crushed or
  finely sliced
250 g uncooked prawn tails,
  shelled and de-veined
1 courgette, cut into matchsticks
1 carrot, finely sliced
1 cup frozen peas
2 tablespoons light soy sauce
4 spring onions, finely
  sliced lengthways
4 tablespoons ready-fried
  onion flakes

Cook the rice in boiling water for 10 minutes. Drain well, and set aside. Heat 1 tablespoon of the oil in a frying pan and fry the beef over high heat to seal – do not cook it fully. Transfer to another plate. Set aside. Using a fork, beat the eggs with the chilli and salt. Add 1 tablespoon of oil to the frying pan, pour in half the egg mixture, adding a little more oil if needed, and make a thin omelette. Turn it over and cook until pale gold on both sides. Make a second omelette with the remaining mixture. Roll both omelettes up, slice finely and set aside. Heat 2 tablespoons of the remaining oil in a large wok or deep frying pan, add the onions and garlic and fry for 3–4 minutes until cooked and dry. Add the remaining 2 tablespoons of oil, the meat, prawns, courgette, carrot and peas. Stir-fry for 2 minutes. Add the rice and sliced omelette. Mix well, then sprinkle with soy sauce. Cover and cook briefly to reheat all ingredients, sprinkling in a little water as needed to help stop sticking. Scatter over the spring onions and onion flakes and serve.

SERVES 4

Pumpkin and
smoked chicken risotto

6 cups liquid chicken stock
¼ cup olive oil
1 onion, diced
2 cloves garlic, crushed
1 red capsicum, de-seeded and finely chopped
500 g arborio rice
500 g pumpkin, peeled
1 cup dry white wine
500 g smoked chicken
½ cup freshly grated parmesan cheese
salt and freshly ground black pepper

Bring stock to the boil in a saucepan. Heat oil in a heavy-based, deep-sided frying pan. Cook onion, garlic and red capsicum for 5 minutes. Add rice and stir over a low heat for 2–3 minutes to toast the rice. Add the pumpkin and wine and cook for 1 minute. Ladle over sufficient boiling stock to just cover the rice. Cook, stirring frequently, adding more stock to cover the rice as the liquid is absorbed. This will take about 25 minutes. Add the smoked chicken at the end and stir until warmed through. Remove pan from the heat. Add parmesan to the pan. Season to taste. Stir to combine. Serve immediately.

SERVES 4

Spaghetti and meatballs

SAUCE
1 tablespoon oil
1 clove garlic, crushed
1 onion, finely diced
400 g can tomatoes in juice
¼ cup tomato paste
salt and freshly ground
    black pepper

MEATBALLS
500 g lean beef mince
2 tablespoons tomato sauce
1 onion, finely diced
1 clove garlic, crushed
1 teaspoon curry powder
½ cup soft breadcrumbs

500 g packet spaghetti, cooked

SAUCE
Heat oil in a saucepan. Add garlic and onion. Cook until golden. Purée tomatoes in juice. Add to pan. Bring to the boil. Stir in tomato paste. Reduce heat and simmer for 10–15 minutes or until thickened to a sauce consistency. Season with salt and pepper to taste and keep warm until meatballs are ready.

MEATBALLS
Preheat oven to 200°C. Put mince, tomato sauce, onion, garlic, curry powder and breadcrumbs in a bowl. Mix thoroughly. Measure tablespoonfuls of mixture and shape into balls. Place on a baking tray or in a shallow ovenproof dish. Cook in oven for 8–10 minutes, until cooked through. To serve, add hot meatballs to the prepared sauce and coat. Spoon on top of cooked spaghetti.

SERVES 4–6

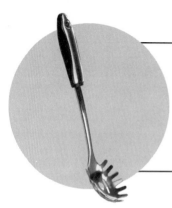

How to cook perfect white rice

There are many types of rice. Long-grain rice has slender polished grains that cook easily and the grains are quite separated. Easy-cook or pre-cooked rices are grains that have been pre-treated and steamed so that the grains remain firm and separate after cooking. Basmati rice is another long grain valued for its fragrant perfume and delicate taste. When cooked the slender grains swell only lengthwise, resulting in thin dry grains perfect for pilafs.

For one person, use ½ cup uncooked rice. Wash rice grains in a sieve in cold water. Run the water through it until the water runs clear and the white starch has gone. Some people choose not to wash rice. The main benefit is to make the grains light and fluffy and remove any dust or grit.

Pan of water cooking
Add rice to a large quantity of boiling water or stock, the more liquid the better. Cook, uncovered, until rice is tender, about 10–15 minutes.

Absorption cooking
Arborio rice is best used for this method as this fat, short grain has a high starch content. When absorbing water it creates a creamy texture. Cover rice with water or stock. Bring to the boil uncovered. Then cover and reduce heat. Avoid lifting the lid. Leave for 10–15 minutes. Risottos are cooked this way and the meaty stock gives rice more flavour.

Cooking rice in a microwave
Choose a large non-metal microwave-proof bowl. For every ½ cup rice, add 500 ml water. Cook, covered, on High for about 10 minutes (time may vary slightly depending on microwave type). Let the rice stand for 5 minutes, after removing from oven and before uncovering. Test to check that rice is cooked by squeezing it between your fingers. The rice should squash but have a slightly harder core. When cooked, rinse rice under hot water. Drain well.

Oven cooking
Place rice in a casserole dish. Add 2 cups of boiling water for each cup of rice. Cover and cook at 180°C for 35–40 minutes.

Pan steaming
Place rice in a saucepan. Add 2 cups of cold water for each cup of rice. Bring to the boil. When holes appear on the surface of the rice, turn down to a low heat and cover with a lid. Steam cook for 15–20 minutes or until water is absorbed and rice cooked.

Brown rice
Brown rice is the least processed form of rice. It has the outer hull removed but retains the nutritious, high-fibre bran layers that give it its light tan colour, nutty flavour and chewy texture. Cook brown rice in boiling water for about 40 minutes or until tender. The husk is coarser in brown rice, so usually takes twice as long as other rice types.

Hint: For the lightest texture, allow cooked rice to stand for 5 minutes before fluffing with a fork and serving.

Main meals with meat

We need protein in our everyday diet for maintenance of our bodies. Lean meats and seafood are the best way to get necessary proteins. Meats provide us with a rich source of iron as well as zinc and other minerals.

Choose meats with less fat and choose to cook them with less fat. Place racks under meat cuts when cooking them in the oven to catch the fat in an oven tray. Baste cuts of meat with water instead of fat to stop them drying out. And use fresh sauces to serve the meat instead of fatty gravies or buttery sauces.

There is nothing more delicious than a well-cooked piece of meat. Whether it is pork, chicken or beef, it needn't be expensive if you have smaller pieces of good-quality meat. Choose a reputable source to buy your meats. They must be well chilled, freshly packed and have been stored properly.

Aim to improve your repertoire in meat cooking. Restricting yourself to just barbecuing, or marinating until there is no meat flavour left, can be very boring. Cooked properly in its own juices, a good cut of meat remains moist, succulent and retains all the essential goodness your body needs.

Steak and mushroom potato top pie, page 64

Spicy beef and noodle stir-fry, page 65

Five ways
with salami

Salami roll-ups
Lay salami pieces flat on chopping board. In a small bowl, mix cream cheese with 1 tablespoon chopped capers. Season well with salt and pepper. Spread the cream cheese mixture over the salami slices and then roll up like cigars. Leave to chill before serving.

Salami pizzas
Spread tomato purée or relish over pre-made pizza bases. Lay salami slices over the relish and top with mozzarella or grated cheese. Cook in hot oven for 10–15 minutes or until cheese has melted. Serve with fresh rocket leaves and freshly ground black pepper.

Salami and couscous
Place 1 cup dried couscous into a bowl. Add 1 cup hot water and allow to absorb. Fluff up the grains with a fork. Finely slice 3–4 dried apricots, a handful of almonds, 5–6 pieces of salami and 2 spring onions. Mix through the couscous. Add grated rind and juice of 1 orange. Season well with salt and pepper and sprinkle over some extra virgin olive oil. Toss together well and serve warm or cold.

Salami and sage potatoes
Preheat oven to 200°C. Peel and dice 6 large potatoes. Place in roasting dish. Sprinkle over sea salt and 2 cloves garlic, roughly chopped. Shred 3–4 sage leaves and toss through the potatoes. Cook for 30 minutes. Dice 200 g salami sausage and add to potato, cook for a further 10–15 minutes, until the potatoes are tender and the oil starts to come out of the salami.

Salami salad
Toss together 1 sliced telegraph cucumber, 4 large diced tomatoes, 1 red onion, cut into thin half rings, a handful of black olives, 200 g salami sausage, cut into cubes, and fresh mesclun lettuce leaves. Top with cubes of feta cheese. Sprinkle over olive oil, balsamic vinegar and season well with salt and pepper.

Main meals
with meat

Beef

Steak and mushroom potato top pie

1 kg beef, e.g. blade or topside steak
2 tablespoons olive oil
1 medium onion, chopped coarsely
3 cloves garlic, crushed
200 g mushrooms, quartered
¼ cup Champion Standard Grade Flour
1½ cups liquid beef stock
½ cup red wine
1 tablespoon Worcestershire sauce
1 tablespoon Dijon mustard
400 g can crushed tomatoes
1.5 kg potatoes, peeled
½ cup milk
50 g butter
salt and freshly ground black pepper

Dice the steak into 2-cm cubes. Heat half of the oil in a large heavy-based pan. Cook the steak, in batches, until well browned all over. Remove from the pan. Heat the remaining oil in the same pan. Cook the onion, garlic and mushrooms, stirring, until soft. Add the flour. Cook, stirring for one minute. Gradually stir in the stock and wine, Worcestershire sauce and mustard, then return the steak to the pan. Add the undrained crushed tomatoes. Bring to the boil and simmer, covered, for 1 hour, stirring occasionally. Remove the lid and continue to cook for 15–20 minutes until the steak is tender and the sauce begins to thicken. Preheat oven to 190°C.

Meanwhile, boil, steam or microwave the potatoes until soft, then drain. Mash the potatoes with the milk, butter and season to taste, until light and fluffy. Spoon the beef mixture into a 2.5 litre (10-cup capacity) ovenproof dish. Top with the hot mashed potato mixture. Place in oven for 30 minutes and then grill for about 5 minutes or until the top is browned.

SERVES 6

Spicy beef
and noodle stir-fry

375 g packet dried egg noodles
2 tablespoons peanut oil
500 g minced beef
4 spring onions, chopped coarsely
3 fresh red chillies, seeds removed and finely chopped
2 cloves garlic, crushed
2 bok choy, quartered
¼ cup soy sauce
¼ cup oyster sauce
1 teaspoon five spice powder

Place the dried noodles in a large bowl of boiling water and stand for 5 minutes or until the noodles are just tender, then drain. Meanwhile, heat half the oil in a wok or a large frying pan. Stir-fry the mince in batches until browned. Remove the mince from the wok. Heat the remaining oil in the wok, add the onion, chilli, garlic and bok choy and stir-fry until the green vegetables are wilted. Return the mince to the wok with the sauces, five spice powder and noodles, then stir-fry until heated through. Serve immediately.

SERVES 4

Beef

Roast beef with Yorkshire pudding

2 kg rolled sirloin, rump or topside roast
1 tablespoon Champion Standard Grade Flour
1 tablespoon mustard powder
salt and freshly ground black pepper

YORKSHIRE PUDDING
1 cup Champion Standard Grade Flour
½ teaspoon salt
1½ cups milk
2 eggs
3 tablespoons hot fat (from beef)

RED WINE GRAVY
½ cup red wine
2½ cups liquid beef stock

Preheat oven to 220°C. Place the beef in a roasting tin, with the thickest part of the fat turned upwards. In a small bowl, mix the flour with the mustard powder and season with salt and pepper. Rub the mixture over the meat. Put the roasting tin in the middle of the oven for 30 minutes. Remove from oven and baste with the juices from the meat. Return to oven and reduce heat to 180°C and continue to cook for about 1 hour, basting occasionally.

When meat is cooked place the beef on another dish, cover loosely with foil and leave to rest in a warm place while cooking the Yorkshire pudding and the gravy. Keep the pan juices and fat.

To make the Yorkshire pudding, sift the flour and salt into a bowl. Mix in half the milk, then add the eggs and season to taste. Beat until smooth, then whisk in remaining milk.

Increase the oven temperature to 220°C. Use 3 tablespoons of beef fat from the beef roasting pan to grease another smaller roasting pan. Heat this pan in the oven for 5 minutes or until the fat is so hot that it is almost smoking. Pour the batter into tin. Bake for 15–20 minutes, until well risen, golden and crisp.

To make the gravy, skim off any remaining fat from the beef roasting tin and discard. Pour in the wine and boil on an element until very syrupy and the sediment on the bottom of the tin starts to come away. Pour in the stock, stir, and bring to the boil until reduced. Season to taste.

Carve beef into slices and serve with gravy, Yorkshire pudding and steamed vegetables.

SERVES 8

Beef

Corned beef
with mustard sauce

1 kg corned silverside
1 bay leaf
sprig parsley
4 black peppercorns
1 tablespoon golden syrup or
    brown sugar
1 thinly peeled strip orange rind
1 tablespoon malt vinegar

MUSTARD SAUCE
1 egg
2 tablespoons sugar
1 tablespoon Champion Standard
    Grade Flour
2 teaspoons mustard powder
1 cup water or the liquid corned
    beef was cooked in
¼ cup malt vinegar
salt and freshly ground
    black pepper

Put silverside in a large saucepan with a lid. Add bay leaf, parsley, peppercorns, golden syrup or sugar, orange rind and vinegar. Barely cover the meat with water. Cover and bring to the boil then simmer gently for 1 hour or until meat is tender. Drain, reserving some liquid for mustard sauce. Serve hot or cold with mustard sauce and steamed vegetables.

To make mustard sauce, beat egg and sugar together. Put into a saucepan. Add flour and mustard powder. Stir in water and vinegar gradually. Cook over a low heat until mixture thickens. Season with salt and pepper to taste, adding more sugar if necessary. Makes 1½ cups.

SERVES 8–10

Main meals
with meat

Beef

Beef and vegetable
casserole

1.5 kg beef blade steak
2 tablespoons olive oil
½ cup balsamic vinegar
2 cups red wine
410 g can tomato purée
3 cups liquid beef stock
5 cups water

4 cloves garlic, crushed
1 teaspoon ground cumin
2 large onions, peeled and sliced
500 g frozen broad beans, peeled
salt and freshly ground
   black pepper

Dice beef into 3-cm cubes. Heat oil in a large heavy-based pan. Cook beef, in batches, until well browned, then remove from pan and keep covered. Add vinegar and wine to the pan and stir until reduced by half. Return beef to pan with tomato purée, stock, water, garlic and cumin. Bring to the boil and simmer, covered, for 2 hours. Transfer beef mixture to a heatproof casserole dish. If possible, cool and chill over-night to remove the layer of fat easily. Return mixture to pan and bring to the boil. Add onions and simmer, uncovered, for about one hour or until tender. Stir in the beans and simmer, uncovered, until hot. Season to taste and serve.

SERVES 6

Thai red beef curry

1 tablespoon oil
1 clove garlic, crushed
2 teaspoons crushed root ginger
3 tablespoons Thai red curry paste
175 g button mushrooms, halved
3–4 spring onions, sliced
225 g green beans, trimmed and halved
500 g sirloin steak, cut into thin strips
400 g can coconut milk
½ cup liquid beef stock
4 tablespoons oil
½ medium onion, sliced
3 tablespoons chopped fresh coriander

Heat oil in a wok. Add garlic, ginger and curry paste and cook for 2 minutes. Add the mushrooms, spring onions and beans and cook for 2–3 minutes. Add beef, cook for 1–2 minutes until brown. Add coconut milk and stock, bring to the boil and reduce by half or until thick and syrupy. Meanwhile, heat second measure of oil in a small pan. Deep-fry onion for 1–2 minutes or until crispy. Drain on absorbent paper. Stir coriander into curry and serve immediately with basmati rice. Garnish with fried onion.

SERVES 4

Beef stroganoff

500 g beef rump steak
25 g butter
1 tablespoon olive oil
1 onion, sliced
150 g mushrooms, sliced
¼ cup white wine
¾ cup sour cream
1 tablespoon lemon juice
salt and freshly ground black pepper
500 g cooked fettuccine, to serve

Trim fat from meat. Cut meat into thin strips. Heat butter and oil in a frying pan. Add meat and quickly brown on both sides. Remove from pan and set aside. Add onion and mushrooms to pan. Cook for 5 minutes until onion is clear. Return meat to pan. Add wine and sour cream. Reheat gently but do not boil. Add lemon juice. Season with salt and pepper to taste, and serve on a bed of fettuccine.

SERVES 4

Main meals
with meat

Beef

Oxtail stew

- 1 kg oxtail pieces
- 1 cup Champion Standard Grade Flour
- 2 tablespoons olive oil
- 2 onions, sliced thinly
- 2 cloves garlic, crushed
- 2 carrots, peeled and sliced
- 2 celery stalks, sliced
- 400 g can whole peeled tomatoes
- 1 tablespoon tomato purée
- 2½ cups liquid beef stock
- 2 teaspoons dried oregano
- salt and freshly ground black pepper
- 12 black olives (optional)

Preheat oven to 160°C. Trim the oxtail of excess fat and coat the pieces with flour. Heat the oil in a heavy-based frying pan. Fry the oxtail pieces in the oil until evenly browned all over. Transfer to a large ovenproof casserole. Fry the onions and garlic in the same oil until lightly coloured then add to the casserole with the carrots, celery, tomatoes, tomato purée, stock, oregano and plenty of seasoning. Cover and cook in oven for 3 hours. If possible, cool and chill overnight to remove the layer of fat easily. If not, spoon off all the fat from the surface before continuing. Add the olives, check the seasoning, and return the casserole to the oven for 1 hour before serving.

SERVES 4

Lamb kebabs with mint sauce, page 74

Lamb tagine, page 75

How to
cook a steak

To cook a perfect beef steak, you need to follow a few simple rules every time. A beef steak can be grilled on a barbecue hot plate, heavy-based frying pan or ribbed cast-iron grill pan.

Choosing a beef steak
Fillet steak is the most tender of cuts of meat and tends to be expensive. But from a good supplier, it is the most rewarding cut of meat, with usually less fat and better texture. Fillet steaks are best for fine dining. Sirloin steaks tend to have more fat in a strip and throughout the grain of meat. Sirloins should be less expensive than the fillet and are ideal for general grill cooking. Rib-eye steaks are tender like the fillets but carry more fat. Rib-eye or rump steak is better for barbecuing on a hot plate.

Cheaper cuts of meat such as T-bones, flank, blade or topside need tenderising with marinades or a meat hammer, to make them tender and palatable. Long cooking times also help a cheaper meat. Therefore, for the best steak, choose good quality and the cooking time will be reduced.

Some fat in the meat keeps the meat juicy while it cooks. Too much fat can turn a healthy meal into a grease trap. When choosing a piece of meat avoid meat that looks reddish grey to brown. Beef steaks that don't smell 'meaty' are fresher. Too much blood coming from the steak means the cut hasn't been butchered properly.

Portion size
A 100–200 g piece of beef is usually a good size for any diner. Too big and the meat can be wasted.

Tenderising steaks
A less expensive meat cut that needs tenderising can be placed between 2 pieces of plastic wrap and pounded with a rolling pin. Alternatively, use a marinade made with red wine, oil, herbs and garlic. Leave steaks to marinate overnight.

Cooking steaks

Steaks are best cooked at room temperature. This allows the meat to relax before putting it onto a hot grill plate. If leaving any meat out of the refrigerator, make sure it is covered well.

Preheat a cast-iron pan, or heavy-bottomed pan or the grill plate until smoking. Lightly oil the pan with a good oil that can take a high temperature – for example, canola, rice bran or peanut. Don't use too much oil, as this will create unnecessary smoke. Place each steak on the preheated plate. Do not crowd the pan or surface. Leave the steaks to cook through on one side (see cooking times below). Do not turn the steaks before one side is properly browned. Turn and then leave steaks to cook through on the other side. Try not to turn again. Tossing them over in the pan toughens the meat unnecessarily.

For the best results grilling or frying sirloin, rump, or fillet steak:

Rare	2½ minutes each side
Medium	4 minutes each side
Well done	6 minutes each side

Testing for perfection

A great way of testing whether your steak is cooked to perfection is by touching it. If it is still soft and spongy then it is on the rare side. When it begins to get firm then it is medium and a very firm steak is well cooked.

Hint: Always allow your steak to stand before serving. Remove from the grill or frying pan and rest, covered, on a warm plate. This allows the steak to 'relax' after the excitement of cooking and therefore produces tender meat.

Lamb

Lamb chops
with ginger marinade

- 8 lamb loin chops
- 2 tablespoons oil
- 2 tablespoons light soy sauce
- 1 clove garlic, crushed
- 2 teaspoons grated root ginger
- 1 tablespoon vinegar
- ½ red chilli, finely chopped
- 1 teaspoon brown sugar
- salt and freshly ground black pepper

Trim chops of excess fat and skin. Combine remaining ingredients in a bowl or jug. Place the chops in a ceramic dish and pour over the marinade. Allow to stand for at least 20 minutes, turning once. Drain the chops, keeping the marinade for later use. Heat a ribbed grill pan or preheat an oven grill. Brush the rack or hot plate with a little oil, grill chops for 2 minutes on each side. Lower heat and continue to cook for a further 4–5 minutes, brushing several times with the marinade. Allow to stand for 5 minutes before serving. Accompany with grilled tomatoes and a baked jacket potato.

SERVES 4

Lamb

Lamb kebabs
with mint sauce

500 g lean lamb
2 cloves garlic, crushed
juice of 1 lemon
1 tablespoon olive oil
2 teaspoons Dijon mustard
2 teaspoons fresh rosemary, chopped
2 small courgettes

1 red onion
16 button mushrooms
1 tablespoon olive oil
8 bamboo skewers

MINT SAUCE
¼ cup mint jelly
1 cup unsweetened yoghurt

Dice lamb into 2-cm cubes. Place lamb, garlic, lemon juice, oil, mustard and rosemary in a bowl. Cover and refrigerate for 1 hour. Cut courgettes into quarters. Cut onion into 8 wedges. Soak bamboo skewers in cold water for 20 minutes. Thread lamb, courgette, mushrooms and onion alternately onto 8 skewers. Heat extra oil in a grill pan or grill plate. Cook kebabs on both sides until lamb is browned and cooked, about 3 minutes each side. Serve kebabs with Mint Sauce and couscous or Tabbouleh (page 43).

SERVES 4

Greek lamb koftas

500 g lean lamb mince
2 teaspoons garlic, crushed
1 teaspoon ground cumin
½ teaspoon ground coriander
2 tablespoons chopped fresh oregano

¼ cup chopped fresh parsley
salt and freshly ground black pepper
8 bamboo skewers
oil to brush

Combine all the ingredients in a bowl. Mix well. Brush the base of a roasting dish with oil. Soak bamboo skewers in cold water for 20 minutes before using. Take spoonfuls of mince mixture and roll into balls. Press the balls onto a bamboo skewer, stretching it out down the skewer. Lay the skewers on a baking tray lined with baking paper. Brush top of the skewers with oil. Preheat oven grill. Grill skewers, 10 cm from heat source, for about 8 minutes, turning once during cooking. Serve immediately.

SERVES 4

Lamb tagine

4 tablespoons olive oil
700 g lamb neck fillet, cut into
    2-cm cubes
2 cloves garlic
1 red onion, sliced
1 red chilli, seeds removed and
    finely chopped
1 teaspoon paprika
2 teaspoons ground cumin
1 cup dried apricots, sliced
1 cinnamon stick
1 cup almonds, whole or flaked
4 cups liquid chicken stock
150 g Greek yoghurt
1 bunch fresh coriander leaves,
    roughly chopped

Heat half the oil in a large frying pan. Add half the meat and cook for 5 minutes, stirring occasionally until browned. Remove from frying pan using a slotted spoon. Fry remaining meat and add to other cooked meat. Add remaining oil and garlic and onion to pan and fry for 4–5 minutes until clear. Stir in chilli, paprika and cumin. Fry for 2 minutes, then stir in the lamb, apricots, cinnamon and almonds. Pour over the stock and season well. Lower heat and simmer for 1 hour until the meat is tender. Remove the cinnamon stick and stir in the yoghurt and all but a little of the coriander. Serve with couscous and garnish with remaining coriander.

SERVES 4

Irish stew

1 kg hogget shoulder chops,
    fat removed
6 medium potatoes, peeled
    and sliced
3 onions, sliced
3 carrots, peeled and sliced
2 cups liquid beef stock
salt and freshly ground
    black pepper
1 tablespoon chopped fresh parsley

Put chops, potatoes, onions, carrots and beef stock into a large saucepan. Cover, bring to the boil. Reduce heat and simmer for 1½ hours or until meat is tender. Season with salt and pepper, to taste. Garnish with parsley.

SERVES 4–6

Main meals
with meat

Lamb

Lamb shanks
in red wine gravy

½ cup Champion Standard Grade Flour
salt and freshly ground black pepper
8 lamb knuckles or shanks
2 tablespoons olive oil
1 onion, finely diced
1 clove garlic, crushed
1½ cups red wine
¼ cup tomato purée
2 cups liquid beef stock
1 tablespoon Edmonds Fielder's Cornflour
1 tablespoon water
3 sprigs rosemary + extra sprigs, to garnish

Preheat oven to 150°C. Place flour in a shallow dish. Season flour with salt and pepper. Trim excess fat from knuckles and discard. Roll knuckles in the flour mixture to coat. Heat oil in a large, heavy-based frying pan. Cook 4 knuckles at a time, turning occasionally until browned. Transfer to a roasting pan. Repeat with remaining knuckles. Cover roasting dish and bake in oven for 1 hour. Remove dish from oven and pour off any fat. While knuckles are cooking, add onion to the frying pan and cook for 5 minutes until soft. Add garlic, wine, tomato purée and stock. Mix cornflour to a paste with water. Add to pan, stirring constantly until sauce thickens slightly and comes to the boil. Season. Pour over knuckles. Lay rosemary on top. Cover dish tightly with foil. Bake for 2 hours, turning knuckles occasionally. Serve with mashed potato or a combination of mashed potato and mashed kumara. Garnish with sprigs of rosemary.

SERVES 4

Boston baked beans, page 82

Barbecue pork spare ribs, page 82

Lamb and prune casserole

1 cup prunes, stones removed
1 cup boiling water
2 tablespoons Champion Standard Grade Flour
1 teaspoon ground cumin
1 teaspoon ground coriander
1 teaspoon ground cinnamon
salt and freshly ground black pepper

750 g lean lamb, diced
1 tablespoon oil
2 onions, finely diced
2 teaspoons Edmonds Fielder's Cornflour
1 tablespoon water
¼ cup sliced almonds, to garnish
coriander leaves, to garnish

Place prunes in a bowl. Pour over water and allow to soak for 30 minutes. Combine flour, spices, salt and pepper in a bowl. Add lamb and toss until evenly coated. Transfer to a casserole dish. Heat oil in a frying pan. Cook onion for 5 minutes until soft. Transfer to casserole dish. Add prunes and water and stir well. Cover dish and bake at 180°C for 1–1½ hours until tender, adding a little more water if all the liquid is absorbed. Mix cornflour to a smooth paste with the water. Stir into meat, then cover and cook for a further 15 minutes. Garnish with almonds and coriander leaves. Serve with mashed potatoes and seasonal vegetables.

SERVES 4

How to
roast a leg of lamb

To invest in a leg roast and to cook it to perfection is a time-honoured tradition. It can feed many and cold leftovers make perfect sandwiches.

You will need
1.5–3 kg lamb leg roast
rosemary sprigs
6–8 cloves garlic, sliced thinly
½ cup olive oil

How to choose a roast
Look for a nice piece of red meat, no dried edges, and not too much fat. Select lamb that is light red in colour. Darker meat is from an older animal and will have a stronger flavour. The fat on lamb should be white, firm and waxy. Organic lamb is perfect, but expensive. A good butcher will trim the leg for you or even remove the bone, so the meat can be rolled out.

How to prepare the meat
Trim any excess fat from the lamb. But remember that fat gives lamb its succulence when cooked and helps to stop the meat from drying out, so don't remove too much. Make about a dozen 1-cm incisions in the top of the fat and meat. Insert a rosemary sprig and piece of garlic. Rub salt and pepper over the top and drizzle with a little olive oil, which helps crispen up the fat layer.

Cooking the meat
Preheat the oven to 170°C. Place the lamb, fat side up, on a rack in a large roasting tin. As a rule, roast lamb is better cooked until slightly pink and medium rare. Using a meat thermometer is ideal, but if you don't have one try these cooking times. For every 500 g of the roast calculate the following for cooking time, plus an extra 20 minutes at the end:

Meat	Time to roast 500 g	Meat thermometer temperature
Medium rare	20–30 minutes	59.9°C
Medium	25–30 minutes	67°C
Well done	35–40 minutes	69°C

Carving the roast
When cooked, remove from oven and cover with tinfoil or the lid of the roasting dish. Leave the roast in a warm place for 10–15 minutes before carving. This allows the meat to 'set' and makes it easier to carve. Use a really sharp carving knife. Hold the meat with a carving fork. Cut across the fibres and the meat will appear to be more tender. Make a cut straight down to the bone lengthways through the middle. Then cut slightly slanting slices at the thinnest part of the roast, finishing at the broadest part of the leg. Make sure that the slices are always across the grain of the meat.

To serve
Serve roast lamb with Mint Sauce (page 74), mint jelly or gravy.

Gravy
1 tablespoon fat in roasting dish
1½–3 tablespoons Champion Standard Grade Flour
1 cup water, stock or vegetable water
salt and freshly ground black pepper

Pour off fat from roasting dish, leaving 1 tablespoon. Sprinkle flour into pan. Use 1½ tablespoons for thin gravy and up to 3 tablespoons for thick gravy. Lightly brown the flour over a medium heat. Add the water slowly, stirring constantly. Stir until boiling. Season with salt and pepper to taste. Pour into a warmed gravy boat or jug.

Pork and bacon

Spanish sausage
casserole

1 tablespoon olive oil
450 g chorizo or spicy sausage, sliced
1 onion, sliced into half rings
4 cloves garlic, crushed
1 tablespoon paprika
salt and freshly ground black pepper
½ cup red wine
400 g can crushed tomatoes
1 tablespoon sugar
2 green capsicums, seeds removed and roughly chopped
1 teaspoon chopped fresh thyme

Heat the olive oil in a large ovenproof dish and add the sausage. Cook over a high heat for 2–3 minutes to seal and lightly brown. Add the onion, garlic, paprika, salt and black pepper to the pan, reduce the heat and cook for a further 5 minutes, until onion has softened. Stir in the wine and tomatoes, and bring to the boil. Reduce heat, then simmer uncovered for 15 minutes. Add the sugar, capsicums and thyme, stir well and cook for a further 20 minutes. Serve at once with crusty bread or chunky roast potatoes.

SERVES 4

Pork and prunes

2 tablespoons olive oil
25 g butter
1 onion, finely diced
4 boneless pork chops

1½ cups cream
12 stoneless ready-to-eat prunes, cut in half

Put the olive oil and butter into a hot frying pan, then add the onion and cook for 3 minutes. Place the pork chops in the pan and cook them over a high heat for 10 minutes, or until the onions are just beginning to brown and the pork chops are sealed on both sides. Stir in the cream and scatter the prunes in the pan. Continue to cook over a gentle heat, for 15 minutes. Remove the pork, place on a serving plate and spoon over the sauce.

SERVES 4

Potato bacon frittata

2 medium potatoes, peeled and chopped
4 bacon rashers, thinly sliced
2 cloves garlic, crushed
1 small leek, thinly sliced
250 g button mushrooms, sliced
2 medium tomatoes, chopped
8 eggs

½ cup milk
1 tablespoon chopped fresh parsley
½ cup grated cheddar cheese
⅓ cup grated fresh parmesan cheese
fresh herbs, to garnish

Boil, steam or microwave potatoes until tender. Drain well. Heat a large non-stick frying pan. Add bacon and cook until slightly crisp. Add garlic, leek and mushrooms. Cook, stirring, until leek is tender. Add tomatoes and cook until most of the liquid is evaporated. Spread potato mixture evenly over base. Whisk eggs, milk and parsley in a large jug and pour over mixture in pan. Cook over medium heat until egg mixture is almost set and lightly browned underneath. Sprinkle cheeses over top. Place pan under a heated grill. Cook until cheese is melted and lightly browned. Garnish with fresh herbs. Cut into wedges. Serve warm or cold.

SERVES 6

Main meals
with meat

Pork and bacon

Boston baked beans

2 tablespoons olive oil
8 rashers bacon, rind removed and chopped
1 large onion, roughly chopped
2 tablespoons Champion Standard Grade Flour
1¼ cups liquid chicken stock
400 g can crushed tomatoes
2 teaspoons Dijon mustard
3 teaspoons brown sugar
3 tablespoons tomato purée
1 tablespoon Worcestershire sauce
420 g can cannellini beans, drained
2 tablespoons sour cream
1 fresh red chilli, sliced (optional)

Heat the oil in a large casserole dish. Add the bacon and cook for 5–6 minutes until browned and crispy. Add the onion to the dish and cook for 3–4 minutes until softened. Stir in the flour and cook for a further minute. Slowly add stock to the dish and bring to the boil. Stir until thickened. Add tomatoes, mustard, sugar, tomato purée, Worcestershire sauce and beans, and cook for a further 1–2 minutes. Season. Bring to the boil, then lower the heat, cover and simmer for 30 minutes to 1 hour, stirring occasionally. Serve with the sour cream and garnish with chilli.

SERVES 4

Barbecue pork spare ribs

½ cup tomato sauce
¼ cup Worcestershire sauce
4 tablespoons mustard
½ teaspoon chilli powder
½ cup brown sugar
salt and freshly ground black pepper
1.5 kg pork spare ribs

Mix together all the ingredients except for ribs. Brush some of the sauce over all the ribs. Leave to marinate for 1 hour or overnight if you can. Preheat oven to 180°C. Place the ribs in a roasting dish lined with baking paper. Cook the ribs in oven for 1 hour, turning during cooking. Brush with sauce mixture every 10 minutes. Heat the rest of the sauce in a small pan for 3 minutes, stirring until heated through. Drizzle the extra sauce over the ribs and serve with garlic bread and a salad.

SERVES 4

Pork and bacon

Pork, apricot
and ginger skewers

1 tablespoon vegetable oil
1 small onion, diced
1 clove garlic, crushed
500 g pork mince
2 tablespoons fresh grated ginger
10 dried apricots, chopped
handful of chopped fresh parsley

1 cup long-grain rice
½ teaspoon turmeric
juice of ½ lemon
150 ml natural
   unsweetened yoghurt
4 skewers, wooden or metal

Preheat oven to 200°C. If using wooden skewers, soak in cold water for 20 minutes.
   Heat the oil in a pan, then fry the onion and garlic for 5 minutes. Allow to cool for 5 minutes, then tip into a bowl with the pork mince, ginger, apricots and half the parsley. Season with salt and pepper. Mould the mixture around skewers, transfer to a roasting tin and cook for 20 minutes. Put the skewers under a hot grill and cook, turning occasionally, for 10 minutes until browned and cooked through. Boil the rice with 600 ml water and the turmeric, covered, for about 12–15 minutes until tender and the water has been absorbed. Stir the rest of the parsley and the lemon into the yoghurt, drizzle over the skewers. Serve with rice.

SERVES 4

Liver and bacon

500 g lamb's fry (liver)
1 tablespoon oil
1 onion, sliced
1½ tablespoons Champion
   Standard Grade Flour

1 cup liquid beef stock
salt and freshly ground
   black pepper
8 rashers bacon, rind removed
parsley

Remove skin then thinly slice the lamb's fry. Heat oil in a frying pan. Add lamb's fry in batches and quickly brown on all sides. Remove from pan. Add onion and cook until golden. Stir in flour and cook 1 minute. Gradually add stock, stirring constantly. Bring to the boil. Season with salt and pepper to taste. Simmer for 5 minutes. Grill the bacon until crisp. Return lamb's fry to pan and continue simmering for about 5 minutes or until just cooked, but still slightly pink. Serve with bacon. Garnish with parsley.

SERVES 6

Main meals
with meat

Pork and bacon

Pork and noodle stir-fry

500 g lean pork schnitzel
3 tablespoons hoisin sauce
¼ cup soy sauce
1 tablespoon honey
2 cloves garlic, crushed
225 g dried egg noodles
2 tablespoons oil

2 onions, thinly sliced
½ cup water
2 bunches bok choy, sliced
1 tablespoon Edmonds Fielder's Cornflour blended with 1 tablespoon water

Cut pork into 1-cm wide strips. Combine hoisin sauce, soy sauce, honey and garlic in a bowl. Add pork and toss to combine. Cover and refrigerate for 1 hour. Cook noodles according to packet instructions. Tip into a sieve and refresh under cold running water. Heat 1 tablespoon of the oil in a wok or heavy-based frying pan. Drain meat from marinade, reserving the marinade. Stir-fry meat for 4–5 minutes until cooked through. Remove from wok. Add remaining oil to wok. Stir-fry onions for 4–5 minutes until soft. Combine reserved marinade and ½ cup water and add to wok. Add pork, cooked noodles and bok choy, tossing over a medium heat for 1–2 minutes until heated through. Mix cornflour to a paste with water. Add to wok, stirring until mixture thickens. Serve immediately.

SERVES 4

Blackened chicken, page 87

Tandoori chicken drumsticks, page 88

Chicken

Mustard chicken loaf

750 g chicken mince
250 g ham, chopped
2 cloves garlic, crushed
4 spring onions, chopped
1 tablespoon fresh rosemary, chopped
1½ cups stale breadcrumbs
1 egg, lightly beaten
1 tablespoon wholegrain mustard
salt and freshly ground black pepper

GLAZE
50 g olive oil spread
1 tablespoon honey
1 tablespoon wholegrain mustard
1 teaspoon finely grated lemon rind

Preheat oven to 180°C. Grease a 14-cm x 21-cm loaf pan and line with baking paper. Combine mince, ham, garlic, spring onions, rosemary, breadcrumbs, egg and mustard in a large bowl. Season well with salt and pepper. Press into prepared pan. Combine all the glaze ingredients in a bowl. Cook loaf in oven for about 30 minutes. Drain off any fat. Turn loaf out onto a baking tray and brush with glaze. Cook for a further 15 minutes, or until cooked through. Serve loaf warm or cold.

SERVES 6-8

Chicken

Indian butter chicken

2 boneless chicken breasts, skin removed
1 tablespoon butter
1 clove garlic, crushed
1 teaspoon grated root ginger
1½ teaspoons garam masala
1 teaspoon ground cumin

300 ml cream
1 teaspoon minced chilli
¼ cup tomato paste
salt and freshly ground black pepper
1 tablespoon chopped fresh coriander or parsley

Cut chicken into 3-cm cubes. Heat butter in a frying pan. Add chicken and brown over moderately high heat. Remove chicken and set aside. Add garlic, ginger and spices to the pan. Cook over low heat, stirring for 1 minute. Add cream, chilli and tomato paste. Bring to the boil. Stir, and leave to simmer for 5 minutes. Add chicken and simmer 10–12 minutes or until chicken is cooked. Season with salt and pepper; sprinkle with coriander or parsley before serving.

SERVES 4

Lemon and apricot chicken

4 boneless chicken breasts, skin removed
¼ cup olive oil
2 lemons, juice only
1 tablespoon brown sugar
1 tablespoon fresh thyme leaves
2 cloves garlic, crushed
2 tablespoons olive oil

1 cup white wine
150 g dried apricots, halved
1 tablespoon Dijon mustard
2 tablespoons chopped fresh tarragon leaves
salt and freshly ground black pepper

Place chicken breasts between two pieces of plastic wrap and beat with a rolling pin until 5–8 mm thick. Mix olive oil, lemon juice, brown sugar, thyme and garlic together in a bowl. Add the chicken and leave to marinate for 3 minutes. Heat oil in a frying pan. Remove chicken from marinade and add to the pan. Fry for 5 minutes until browned, turning once. Add the reserved marinade, wine and apricots and cook for a further 10–15 minutes until cooked through. Remove chicken from pan. Increase heat and boil for 2–3 minutes until sauce is reduced to about half. Stir in the mustard and tarragon and return chicken to the pan. Season to taste.

SERVES 4

Chicken

Blackened chicken

4 boneless chicken breasts, skin removed
25 g butter, melted
1 teaspoon salt
2 teaspoons fresh thyme, chopped
1 teaspoon chilli powder
1 tablespoon cayenne pepper
1 teaspoon crushed peppercorns
1 teaspoon dried garlic
1 teaspoon dried chilli flakes

Brush the chicken pieces all over with butter. Mix the spices together on a plate and roll the chicken in the spices to coat evenly. Cover and refrigerate for 2 hours. Cook the chicken on a hot barbecue for 10 minutes each side or until the juices run clear. Serve with a tomato relish or salsa.

SERVES 4

Citrus and
balsamic-glazed chicken

½ cup freshly squeezed orange juice (juice of 2 oranges)
¼ cup orange marmalade
¼ cup brown sugar
2 tablespoons balsamic vinegar
8 chicken thighs (bone in), or chicken pieces of your choice
cooked rice to serve

Preheat oven to 190°C. Combine orange juice, marmalade and brown sugar in a saucepan. Stir over a low heat until sugar dissolves. Bring to the boil. Remove from heat and stir in vinegar. Place chicken thighs in a single layer in a baking dish. Pour over glaze and toss to coat. Bake in oven for 35–40 minutes or until chicken is cooked through and golden, turning occasionally and spooning glaze over chicken. Serve on a bed of cooked rice. Accompany with a tossed salad or vegetables of your choice.

SERVES 4

Main meals
with meat

Chicken

Parmesan crumbed chicken

4 single boneless chicken breasts, skin removed
1½ cups fresh breadcrumbs
½ cup finely grated parmesan cheese
¼ cup fresh coriander, chopped
salt and freshly ground black pepper
1 egg, lightly beaten
olive oil to drizzle
sweet chilli sauce to serve

Preheat oven to 180°C. Place chicken breasts between two sheets of plastic wrap and beat with a rolling until 1 cm thick. Combine breadcrumbs, cheese, coriander and salt and pepper in a bowl. Dip chicken into egg, draining off excess. Roll in breadcrumb mixture. Place on a lightly greased baking tray. Drizzle with a little oil. Bake in oven for 20–25 minutes or until chicken is cooked through. Serve with sweet chilli sauce and a tossed salad.

SERVES 4

Tandoori chicken drumsticks

12 chicken drumsticks
juice of 1 lemon
1 teaspoon crushed fresh ginger
1 red chilli
2 tablespoons chopped fresh coriander
1½ cups yoghurt
1 teaspoon ground coriander
1 teaspoon ground cumin
1 teaspoon paprika
1 teaspoon garam masala
¼ cup tomato purée
salt and freshly ground black pepper

Using absorbent paper, remove the excess moisture from the chicken drumsticks. In a large bowl mix together the remaining ingredients. Toss the chicken pieces through the paste, coating well. Allow to marinate for 20–30 minutes in the fridge. Preheat oven to 200°C or barbecue grill to medium. Cook the chicken pieces for 20 minutes until the juices run clear. Serve with naan bread and lemon wedges.

SERVES 4

Chicken and mushroom pie

1 tablespoon olive oil
1 onion, finely diced
500 g chicken thighs, diced
3 stalks celery, finely diced
500 g button mushrooms, sliced thinly
125 g butter
¼ cup Edmonds Standard Grade Flour
2½–3 cups milk
2 teaspoons wholegrain mustard
1 teaspoon chicken stock powder
salt and freshly ground black pepper
4 sheets Edmonds Savoury Short Pastry
1 egg, beaten, for brushing

In a large frying pan, heat the oil and cook the onion until softened. Add the chicken pieces and cook for 10 minutes, until juices are clear. Add the celery and mushrooms and cook a further 5 minutes. In another large saucepan, melt the butter. Remove from the heat, and add the flour and stir until well mixed. Return to the heat, and slowly stir in the milk, mixing well with a wooden spoon to dissolve the flour butter mixture. Add the mustard and chicken stock. Season to taste. When the sauce has thickened remove from heat. Stir in the cooked chicken and mushrooms. Mix well. Preheat oven to 180°C. Lightly grease a 25-cm pie dish with butter. Overlap 2 sheets of pastry over the bottom of the dish. Spoon chicken and sauce into the pie dish. Cover with remaining pastry and trim away the excess. Seal the edges with a fork. Make a slit in the top of the pie to allow steam to escape. Brush with beaten egg. Bake in oven for 30 minutes or until pastry is golden brown.

SERVES 6–8

Chicken

Thai chicken curry

2 boneless chicken breasts, skin removed
1 tablespoon peanut oil
1 onion, finely diced
2 cloves garlic, crushed
1 tablespoon prepared green curry paste
425 g can light coconut cream
¼ cup liquid chicken stock
2 tablespoons chopped fresh coriander or parsley
steamed rice for 4
½ cup roasted peanuts (optional)

Cut chicken into 2-cm pieces. Heat oil in a large saucepan. Sauté onion and garlic for 5 minutes or until clear. Add curry paste and sauté for 1 minute or until spices smell fragrant. Add chicken, coconut cream and stock. Cook for 20 minutes or until chicken is cooked. Stir in coriander or parsley. Serve with steamed rice garnished with roasted peanuts.

SERVES 4

Pumpkin and chicken filo pies

300 g pumpkin, seeds removed and diced
1 large potato, diced
1 tablespoon butter
2 tablespoons oil
2 onions, finely diced
2 teaspoons ground cumin
1 teaspoon garam masala
1 single boneless chicken breast, skin removed
1 clove garlic, crushed
1 cup grated tasty cheddar cheese
salt and freshly ground black pepper
50 g butter, melted
18 sheets Edmonds Filo Pastry

Cook the pumpkin and potato in boiling water until tender. Drain. Add the butter and mash well. Heat the oil in a frying pan and cook onion, cumin, garam masala and diced chicken for 6–8 minutes until onion is soft. Add the garlic and cook for 2 minutes. Combine mashed vegetable mixture, chicken mixture and cheese. Season. Brush 12 deep-pan muffin tins with melted butter. For each pie, lightly brush a sheet of filo pastry with melted butter. Fold in half widthways, then brush with butter. Fold in half again. Line prepared tins with the pastry. Spoon the filling into pastry-lined tins. Cut the remaining 6 sheets of filo pastry in half widthways. Scrunch each portion into a ball and place on top of pies. Brush with melted butter. Bake at 190°C for 20 minutes until golden. Stand for 8–10 minutes before serving.

MAKES 12

How to
roast a chicken

A well-roasted chicken is everyone's favourite. Mix it up a little with different flavourings or stuffings, or by placing aromatic herbs and lemons under the skin and in the cavity. To keep chicken moist, pay attention while cooking and keep it basted.

You will need
Size 18 chicken
50 g butter, softened
salt and freshly ground black pepper
1¼ cups liquid chicken stock or hot water

To prepare the chicken
If you have bought a frozen chicken make sure it is properly thawed before roasting. Alternatively, choose a fresh chicken. Rinse the chicken under running water and dry. Rinse out the cavity of the chicken and remove any giblets.

Take the butter and season well, then push the butter between the skin and the flesh, smearing it evenly. This acts as a sort of internal basting mechanism, keeping the chicken moist. To vary the flavour, try adding different herbs and spices to the basting butter.

For a successful roast, the chicken must keep its shape. This stops it drying out and makes it look more appetising. Shape it neatly and tuck the neck flap underneath. Tuck the wings underneath themselves, to stop them from drying out. Wrap tinfoil around the ends of the wings and drumsticks to stop these parts from overcooking or burning.

To cook the chicken
Preheat oven to 190°C. Weigh chicken or read the weight from the packet. Calculate the cooking time: allow 25 minutes per 500 g, plus an extra 20 minutes. Place chicken breast-side down on a roasting rack in roasting pan. This distributes juices evenly during cooking, adding to the flavour. Pour over chicken stock or hot water and then roast. This will give something to baste with and use for gravy. Add more stock if it evaporates too quickly. Roast for 20 minutes, then turn the bird breast-side up.

Basting keeps the meat moist and succulent, so every 20 minutes spoon the juices all over the chicken. When cooking time is up, pierce the thickest part of the thigh with a skewer – if the juices run clear, it's ready. Remove from oven, cover with foil and leave for 10 minutes, so the meat relaxes and the juices are evenly distributed. To garnish, just place a few fresh herbs between the legs.

To carve a roasted chicken

Stick a carving fork in a leg then carve between the leg and the breast, removing the leg completely. Repeat on the other side and with the wings. To carve the breast, either slice it off whole then slice on the diagonal or, with the breast still on the chicken, carve individual slices from the top of the breast down.

Tips for cooking with chicken

The better the quality of bird, the better the roast. Corn-fed or organic chickens may be more expensive but taste far superior in the end.

Chicken and pork are more susceptible to bad bacteria than other meats. Always treat the meat with care.

Always wash your chopping board thoroughly after working with raw chicken and before preparing or cutting cooked chicken or other foods.

Always use the freshest of cuts. Fresh chicken pieces will last in the fridge, covered, for 2–3 days. Smell will be the first thing that will tell you the chicken has gone off.

When defrosting chicken, put pieces in a container, and cover well. Do not place chicken pieces straight into the fridge as blood may spill from a container or drip from a packet.

Chicken is better to be defrosted in a fridge and at a constant temperature. Do not be tempted to use hot water or microwaves for defrosting as any warmth can start microbial growth.

When carving cooked chicken pieces make sure the chopping board and surfaces are well cleaned afterwards.

Salmon risotto cakes, page 94

Crunchy-topped fish fillets, page 98

Fish and shellfish

We are lucky in this country to have an abundance of fish and shellfish. It is available fresh or frozen and in many wonderful varieties.

Always look for the freshest fish. A good supermarket or fish shop should stock the freshest of fish, and you can tell by the smell. A strong odour or smell of ammonia is not a good sign for fish or seafood. If mussels or cockles are half open, chances are they have died – don't buy them. The eyes of a fish should be bright, not cloudy, and the flesh should be firm, not squishy.

As it is plentiful, buy fish fresh on a regular basis. Don't store it in your home fridge for more than 2 days. Your fridge is probably not cold enough for any seafood. Keep the fillets or pieces of seafood well wrapped to prevent dripping on other foods. And, as with chicken, remember to wipe all surfaces that raw seafood comes into contact with.

Most importantly, fish is very good for you. Some oily fish, e.g. salmon and mackerel, are full of valuable Omega-3 fatty acids which are beneficial for heart health. Omega-3 is also considered beneficial for brain development. Include 2–3 meals of fish and seafood in your diet every week – you can't go wrong.

Salmon risotto cakes

50 g butter
2 tablespoons olive oil
1 small onion, finely diced
300 g arborio rice
3½ cups liquid vegetable stock, heated
1 bunch of spring onions, finely chopped
salt and freshly ground black pepper
450 g salmon fillet or 450 g can pink salmon, bones removed
1 egg, lightly beaten

Heat the butter and 1 tablespoon of the oil in a large saucepan, then add the onion and cook for about 5 minutes without browning. Add the rice and stir well to coat the grains. Add the hot stock, a cupful at a time, and stir well. Bring to the boil, then reduce the heat. Simmer, stirring occasionally, for about 20 minutes until the rice is just tender. Stir in the spring onions and season with salt and pepper to taste. Remove from the heat. When the mixture has cooled completely, stir in the salmon and beaten egg. Wet your hands and shape the mixture into 12 rounds. Cover and refrigerate for at least 2 hours. Preheat oven to 180°C. Pour the remaining tablespoon of oil into a large roasting tin and heat in oven for a few minutes. Add the risotto cakes, cook for 10 minutes and turn to coat in the hot oil. Cook a further 10 minutes. Remove from pan and drain on absorbent paper before serving with steamed vegetables.

SERVES 6

Smoked fish kedgeree

250 g smoked fish
50 g butter
1 small onion, finely diced
1 cup cooked long-grain rice
2 hard-boiled eggs
salt and freshly ground black pepper
1 tablespoon chopped fresh parsley

Flake fish and remove any bones. Melt butter in a saucepan. Add onion and cook until clear. Add rice and fish and heat through. Halve eggs and remove yolks and set aside. Chop egg white. Add to saucepan. Season with salt and pepper to taste. When kedgeree is very hot transfer to serving dish. Garnish with parsley and sieved reserved egg yolks.

SERVES 3-4

Spanish paella

6 cups liquid fish or chicken stock
400 g can whole tomatoes in juice
pinch saffron threads or ¼ teaspoon turmeric
1 boneless chicken breast, skin removed
1 green capsicum, seeds removed

3 tablespoons olive oil
2 onions, diced
2 cloves garlic, crushed
3 cups short-grain rice
12 mussels, in shells
6 whole uncooked prawns
4 lemons

Heat the stock, tomatoes and juice, and saffron threads until boiling. Cut chicken into 1-cm strips. Remove core from capsicum and cut flesh into 1-cm cubes. Heat oil in a paella dish or large frying pan. Sauté chicken until lightly browned. Add onions, garlic and capsicum and sauté for 2 minutes. Add rice and stir to coat. Cook until rice becomes transparent. Add the hot stock mixture and stir. Simmer for 10 minutes. Add mussels and simmer for 5 minutes or until mussels open. Discard any that do not open. Add prawns and cook for a further 2 minutes. Add more stock if necessary. Remove from heat. Squeeze the juice of two of the lemons over the top of the paella. Cover and stand for 5 minutes. Cut remaining lemons into quarters and use to garnish paella.

Tip: Turmeric can be used as a substitute for saffron. Use ¼ teaspoon turmeric in this recipe – it gives the same golden colour as saffron.

SERVES 6–8

Creamy garlic mussels

24–48 mussels in shells, washed and scrubbed
1 onion, finely diced
½ cup white wine
25 g butter
4 large cloves garlic, crushed

1 tablespoon Edmonds Fielder's Cornflour
300 ml cream
2 tablespoons fresh parsley, chopped
salt and freshly ground black pepper

Place mussels, onion and wine in a large pan. Cover and cook over high heat for 3–4 minutes or until shells open. Discard any mussels that have not opened. Remove empty half shells and place mussels in a serving bowl. Cover and keep warm. Boil cooking liquid for 3–4 minutes. Strain through a fine sieve then measure ½ cup of the liquid and set aside. Melt butter. Add garlic and cook. Stir in cornflour, then cooking liquid and cream. Bring to the boil, stirring, simmer 3 minutes or until lightly thickened. Add parsley and season well with salt and pepper. Pour sauce over mussels. Serve immediately.

SERVES 4

Stir-fried lemon
and ginger fish

500 g firm white fish fillets, e.g. cod or gurnard, skin removed
1 teaspoon salt
1 tablespoon oil
½ cup frozen peas, cooked
½ cup frozen sweet corn, cooked
⅓ cup liquid chicken stock or water

1 tablespoon grated root ginger
2 teaspoons lemon juice
2 teaspoons soy sauce
1 teaspoon sugar
1 teaspoon Edmonds Fielder's Cornflour, blended with 1 teaspoon water
spring onions, to garnish

Cut fish fillets into 2.5-cm wide strips, sprinkle with the salt and leave for 15 minutes. Heat oil in a frying pan, add the fish and stir-fry for 3 minutes. Add the remaining ingredients, except the blended cornflour, and bring to the boil. Stir in the blended cornflour and cook for 1 minute. Garnish with spring onions and serve immediately with white rice.

SERVES 4

Thai-seasoned
salmon steaks

4 salmon steaks
2 tablespoons sesame oil
½ cup sweet chilli sauce
¼ cup soy sauce
2 tablespoons brown sugar

2 tablespoons tomato sauce
2 tablespoons lemon juice
1 stalk lemon grass, finely chopped (optional)

Brush salmon steaks with oil. Place on a baking tray lined with baking paper. Mix together remaining ingredients. Brush over the salmon steaks. Preheat the grill to high. Grill the salmon for 10 minutes or until salmon is cooked through, turning once during cooking and brushing with more sauce. Serve with steamed bok choy and lemon wedges.

SERVES 4

Fish burgers
with crunchy batter

CRUNCHY BATTER
¼ cup Edmonds Fielder's Cornflour
½ cup Edmonds Standard Grade Flour
1 teaspoon Edmonds Baking Powder
¼ teaspoon salt
½ cup milk

4 firm white fish fillets, e.g. hoki, tarakihi
oil for cooking
4 hamburger buns
4 lettuce leaves
8 tomato slices
8 cucumber slices
8 onion rings
lemon wedges
tartare sauce

Sift cornflour, flour, baking powder and salt into bowl. Gradually add milk, mixing until smooth. Dip the fish to be cooked in the batter, ensuring it is well coated. Deep-fry in hot oil until golden. Drain on absorbent paper. Toast the hamburger buns. Lay lettuce leaves, tomato, cucumber and onion rings on the bun base. Place cooked fish fillets on top with a spoonful of tartare sauce. Serve with lemon wedges.

SERVES 4

Crunchy-topped
fish fillets

3 slices grain bread
1 courgette, grated
50 g parmesan cheese, grated
2 cloves garlic, crushed
zest of 1 lemon

salt and freshly ground
black pepper
4 firm white fish fillets,
e.g. tarakihi, gurnard
or snapper

Preheat oven to 180°C. Make the bread into breadcrumbs by grating or blending in food processor. In a bowl mix the breadcrumbs, grated courgette, cheese, garlic and lemon zest. Season well with salt and pepper. Prepare an ovenproof dish with baking paper and lay the fish fillets on it. Press spoonfuls of the mixture onto the top of each fillet. Bake in oven for 35 minutes until fish is opaque. Serve immediately with salad or fresh steamed vegetables.

SERVES 4

Fish and smoked mussel pie

25 g butter
1 small onion, diced
½ teaspoon curry powder
2 tablespoons Edmonds Standard
    Grade Flour
¾ cup milk

310 g can smoked fish, drained
and flaked
12 smoked mussels, diced
freshly ground black pepper
2 sheets Edmonds Flaky Puff Pastry
1 egg yolk

Preheat oven to 220°C. Melt butter in a saucepan. Add onion and cook until clear. Stir in curry powder. Cook for 30 seconds. Stir in flour and cook until frothy. Gradually add milk, stirring constantly until mixture boils and thickens. Remove from heat. Add fish and mussels and season to taste. Stir, then set aside until cool. Place a sheet of pastry on oven tray. Spread fish mixture over pastry, leaving a 2-cm edge all the way round. Dampen this edge lightly with water. Carefully fold second sheet of pastry in half. From centre fold make 1.5-cm wide cuts to within 2-cm of edge. Open out and carefully lift over filling. Press edges firmly together. Lightly beat egg yolk and brush top surface of pastry with this mixture, making sure egg does not drip down sides as this will prevent pastry from rising. Cook in oven for 20 minutes or until golden and well risen.

SERVES 4-6

How to
cook fish

It is bountiful, and good for you. It doesn't need to be coated in batter and served with chips to make it appealing for dinner. Fish is easy to prepare and tasty.

Grilling
To cook grilled fish with a crisp brown outside and moist, perfectly cooked flesh inside, it is essential to preheat the grill to its highest setting. Steaks, fillets and small whole fish are ideal for grilling, although shouldn't be more than 5 cm thick otherwise the fish will remain cold and raw on the inside.

To grill fish, lay the steaks or fillets on greased foil on the grill rack. Brush the fish with melted butter or a good-quality oil, season lightly and set close to the preheated grill. Herb or spice oils and butters are perfect with any fish to boost the flavour. Fish should be at room temperature before grilling. If fish is too cold or still frozen, it will affect the texture of the fish while cooking. Do not salt the fish as salt draws out moisture. Avoid overcooking the fish, otherwise it will be tough and dry. To know when fish is cooked separate the flakes with a fork and check flesh is flaky.

Cooking time for grilled fish varies with the heat of the grill, the distance of the fish from the heat, the thickness of the cut and its fat content.

Steaming
Steaming is cooking of food over, rather than in, boiling liquid. Steaming is a perfect cooking method for fish. It preserves the delicate flavour of any fillet or cutlet. There is minimal mineral and vitamin loss during cooking.

To steam fish, use oval or round steamers, bought from any store, which are like double saucepans. Chinese bamboo baskets are cheap, easy-to-use steamers and can be bought from any Asian food store. Always use a steamer/saucepan with a close-fitting lid to trap the steam. The fish must be well seasoned before steaming, otherwise it may taste a little bland. The water underneath the steamer should be kept at a constant boil to enable the fish to cook quickly. Prevent putting too much in the steamer, otherwise the fish will cook unevenly.

Steaming is great because vegetables can be used in the same steamer and at the same time, for a quick and nutritious meal.

Baking
Baking fish is usually at about 170°C to 190°C, which is moderately hot. The time it takes usually depends on the cut and thickness of the fish. Lay the fish on a large sheet of lightly oiled aluminium foil or baking paper. Use onion, bay leaf, fennel or lemon rind to flavour the fish. Wrap the fillets up loosely then bake in preheated oven. For example, a filleted small salmon or snapper will take about 30–35 minutes.

Barbecue
For barbecuing choose types of fish that are thick and oily, such as tuna, marlin, salmon or hapuka steaks. Any firm type of fleshed fish can be used. Marinating fish before it goes on the grill is advisable to give flavour and oil to the fish. Apply oil to the fish rather than the grill plate to stop the piece sticking and becoming greasy. Wrapping fish in greased foil is also a good way of preventing the fillets sticking.

Pan-frying
Best suited for small whole fish, fillets, steaks and cutlets and delicate fish. Minimal amounts of fat or oil are needed and when choosing which to use, think about the type of fish, so that the flavour of the fish is not lost. Butter is perfect for fish frying, but the milk solids in butter will burn quickly at high heats. A way to avoid this is to use clarified butter or add a little rice bran or olive oil to the butter.

To pan-fry fish, use an uncovered wide pan. A lid traps the steam and food stews or steams rather than fries. Use a minimal amount of fat and preheat the fat or oil. If the fat is cool, the fish will not brown and will lack flavour and it will absorb too much oil making it too greasy. Fry a little fish at a time. Adding too many pieces at once to a hot pan lowers the temperature quickly and makes the fish greasy. Lightly dusting the fillets in flour or rice flour before cooking helps to prevent sticking and adds crispiness to the fish. Adding garlic or parsley to the pan will help flavour the fish while cooking as well.

Veggie tofu burgers, 105

Silverbeet and feta pie, page 107

Vegetarian dishes

Vegetables, as your mother would say, are good for you. And guess what? They really are! Forget supplements, fibre drinks and special drinks full of antioxidants – vegetables have it all. Packed with vitamins, minerals, antioxidants and fibre, all vegetables are good for you and, when cooked well, they taste good too.

With vegetables in the fridge there is always a meal on hand. For meat eaters, choose to have at least one vegetarian meal a week. (Don't think of it as vegetarian, just don't include meat!) For vegetarians, it is important to include proteins such as cheese, nuts and beans in your diet.

Experiment with new vegetables, such as Asian greens and new varieties, or just enjoy the colourful array of common seasonal vegetables. Growing your own is therapeutic and rewarding but, for those of us with no space and time, a good greengrocer works fine. For the budget-minded, vegetables provide the best way to pad out your weekly grocery spend. Buy them fresh each week. Don't be tempted to buy masses at a time, because they will rot and lose their freshness.

Five ways
with frozen peas

Peas and ginger
Mix together 100 g softened butter with 1 tablespoon grated root ginger. Cook 450 g frozen peas for 5–8 minutes in boiling water. Drain. Add the butter mixture to the peas and heat for a further 2–3 minutes, until butter has melted.

Mushy peas
Cook 450 g frozen peas in boiling water for 8–10 minutes until soft. Drain well. In a frying pan cook 1 onion, diced, on a low heat with 1 tablespoon butter until soft. Add 2 rashers bacon, finely sliced. Add half the peas with another tablespoon butter and cook through for 5 minutes. Remove pan from heat and mash the peas down with a fork. Add the remaining peas and return to heat for 5 minutes.

Minted peas with yoghurt and feta
Cook 450 g frozen peas in boiling water for 8–10 minutes until soft. Drain well and allow to cool. Mix peas with 150 g Greek yoghurt, 1 tablespoon lemon juice, 2 tablespoons sliced fresh mint, salt and pepper to season and 150 g crumbled feta. Stir to combine. Serve garnished with extra mint leaves.

French peas
Melt 1 tablespoon butter in a medium saucepan over a low heat. Add 1 sliced onion and cook, stirring, until onion is soft. Add 1½ cups frozen peas and 2 large sliced lettuce leaves. Stir until lettuce wilts. Add ½ cup liquid chicken stock, 1 teaspoon sugar and 1 teaspoon salt. Bring to the boil, cover and simmer for about 5 minutes or until tender. Serve with grilled or roasted meat.

Pea purée
Cook 450 g peas until tender. Place in a food processor with 150 g crème fraîche and purée. Return to the pan, season well and heat. Sprinkle with dill or flat-leaf parsley to serve.

Vegetable and
cottage cheese lasagne

TOMATO SAUCE
1 tablespoon vegetable oil
1 onion, finely diced
2 x 400 g cans tomatoes in juice
1 clove garlic, crushed
salt and freshly ground
 black pepper
1 medium eggplant

4 courgettes
2 capsicums, any colour
1 tablespoon oil
500 g lasagne sheets
200 g cottage cheese
1½ cups grated cheddar cheese
 or mozzarella cheese

To make the tomato sauce, heat oil in a frying pan. Cook onion for 5 minutes until soft. Add tomatoes and garlic, breaking up tomatoes with a wooden spoon. Simmer for about 25 minutes until sauce is thick. While the sauce is cooking, prepare vegetables.

Preheat oven to 180°C. Trim ends off eggplant and courgettes and dice. Core and seed peppers and dice. Heat oil in a heavy frying pan and cook vegetables until tender. Lay half the lasagne over the base of a 24-cm x 20-cm rectangular ovenproof dish. Top with half the sautéed vegetables, then half the tomato sauce and half the cottage cheese. Repeat these layers, finishing with the sauce. Sprinkle with cheese. Bake in oven for 25–30 minutes. Stand for 5 minutes. Serve with a tossed salad and crusty bread.

SERVES 4

Sweet potato vegetable curry

1 tablespoon oil
50 g butter
1 large onion, sliced
2 cloves garlic, crushed
2 teaspoons grated root ginger
1 tablespoon mustard seeds
2 teaspoons cumin seeds
2 fresh red chillies, chopped
¼ teaspoon ground turmeric
1 tablespoon ground coriander
1 tablespoon tomato paste
1 large kumara, peeled and chopped coarsely
1 red capsicum, seeds removed and chopped coarsely
400 g can tomatoes in juice
1 teaspoon sugar
2½ cups liquid vegetable stock
250 g cauliflower florets
1½ cups frozen peas
¼ cup coarsely chopped fresh coriander

Heat oil and butter in a large saucepan. Add the onion, garlic, ginger, seeds, chillies, turmeric and coriander. Cook, stirring, for about 2 minutes or until fragrant. Add tomato paste, kumara, capsicum, undrained crushed tomatoes, sugar and stock. Bring to the boil, simmer, uncovered, for 10 minutes or until kumara is almost tender. Add the cauliflower florets to the curry, simmer, uncovered, for about 10 minutes or until vegetables are tender. Stir in the peas and simmer, uncovered, for about 2 minutes or until hot. Sprinkle with coriander and serve with rice, if desired.

SERVES 4

Veggie tofu burgers

1 medium carrot, peeled and grated
1 courgette, grated
600 g firm tofu, finely diced
¼ cup fresh coriander leaves, chopped
2 cloves garlic, crushed
2 eggs, lightly beaten
½ cup Champion Standard Grade Flour
3 teaspoons ground cumin
salt and freshly ground black pepper
1 cup Champion Standard Grade Flour
vegetable oil for shallow-frying
6 bread rolls
6 lettuce leaves
2 medium tomatoes, sliced
1 avocado, sliced
mild sweet chilli sauce to serve

Squeeze excess liquid from grated carrot and courgette. Mix the carrot, courgette, tofu, coriander, garlic, eggs, first quantity of flour, cumin and seasonings together well. Divide mixture into 6 portions and shape into patties. Coat with second quantity of flour and shake away excess. Shallow-fry patties in hot oil until browned on both sides and heated through. Drain on absorbent paper. Split and toast bread rolls. Divide lettuce leaves over the bread buns, top with cooked patties, tomato and avocado. Drizzle with sweet chilli sauce.

SERVES 6

Pumpkin and onion flan

4 sheets Edmonds Filo Pastry
2 tablespoons vegetable oil
3 eggs
¾ cup milk
½ cup sour cream
½ teaspoon ground nutmeg
freshly ground black pepper to season
2 onions, sliced
1 cup grated pumpkin
1 cup tasty cheese, grated
1 tablespoon sesame seeds

Preheat oven to 190°C. Lay one sheet of filo pastry on a clean board and brush it with a little oil. Cover with the second sheet and brush it with oil. Continue layering until all the pastry is used. Line a 24-cm-diameter flan dish with the pastry and trim it 2 cm above the top of the flan dish. Beat the eggs, milk, sour cream, nutmeg and pepper together. Place the onion, pumpkin and cheese in the flan dish. Pour in the egg mixture and sprinkle with sesame seeds. Bake in oven for 40–50 minutes or until golden brown and firm to touch.

SERVES 6

Vegetarian dishes

Cheese, tomato
and bread pudding

1 loaf French bread, cut into thin slices
50 g butter, softened
400 g can chopped tomatoes
3 tablespoons freshly chopped oregano
2 cloves garlic, crushed
225 g cheddar cheese, grated
2½ cups milk
4 eggs, large
1 tablespoon Dijon mustard

Preheat oven to 180°C. Spread the bread slices thinly with butter. Arrange half in an oval ovenproof dish. Mix together tomatoes, 2 tablespoons oregano and garlic. Spoon half the tomato mixture into the centre of each bread slice. Sprinkle with half the cheese. Top with remaining bread slices, then with the remaining tomato mixture and cheese. In a jug, mix together the milk, eggs and mustard. Pour evenly and slowly over bread, allowing the mixture to seep in gently. Bake for 35–40 minutes, or until golden and set. Sprinkle with remaining oregano and serve.

SERVES 4

Lentil tart

2 sheets Edmonds Savoury Short Pastry
1½ cups red split peas or lentils
3 cups liquid vegetable stock
1 onion, finely chopped
2 cloves garlic, crushed
salt and freshly ground black pepper
1 tablespoon chopped fresh coriander
1 teaspoon garam masala
1 tablespoon chutney
2 eggs, beaten
6 button mushrooms, sliced
1 tomato, sliced
100 g gruyere cheese, grated

Preheat oven to 190°C. Roll out the pastry to fit a 25-cm fluted flan dish. Trim edges and prick base with a fork. Cover pastry with baking paper and spread with baking beans or rice. Place in oven and bake for 20 minutes. When the pastry base is cooked, remove paper and baking beans or rice and allow to cool. Cook the lentils in the stock with the onion and garlic for 15 minutes, until stock has been absorbed and season well. Stir in the coriander, garam masala, chutney and eggs and spoon into the base of the flan case. Top the lentil mixture with the mushrooms and tomato, and sprinkle on the cheese. Cook in oven for 20–25 minutes until set and golden. Serve warm or cold.

SERVES 4–6

Silverbeet and feta pie

8 stalks silverbeet
4 tablespoons olive oil
1 onion, finely diced
2 cloves garlic, crushed
2 slices bread, cut into cubes
200 g feta cheese
½ cup parmesan cheese, grated
salt and freshly ground black pepper
2 eggs, beaten
4 sheets Edmonds Savoury Short Pastry

Cut out the white central stalks of the silverbeet. Wash leaves well. Cook the silverbeet in a small amount of boiling water. When just tender, drain well by squeezing out any excess water. Chop the cooked silverbeet and set aside.

Preheat oven to 200°C. Heat the oil in a heavy frying pan and fry the onion, garlic and bread for 10 minutes until golden brown. Add onion mixture to the silverbeet and mix together thoroughly. Add the feta cheese, parmesan cheese, seasonings and beaten egg. Mix well. Place ½ the pastry sheets into a tart dish or flan ring. Put in the silverbeet filling. Place the remaining pastry over the tart. Seal the edges together. Brush over with a little milk. Bake in oven for about 20 minutes or until golden brown.

SERVES 6

Vegetarian dishes

Gratin of pumpkin

1 kg buttercup pumpkin, peeled, seeded and diced
400 g potatoes, peeled and diced
2 eggs, beaten
100 g butter, well softened
150 g grated tasty cheese
4 tablespoons grated parmesan cheese
salt and freshly ground black pepper
pinch ground nutmeg
2 tablespoons melted butter

Preheat oven to 180°C. Cook pumpkin in a little salted water either in a saucepan on the stove or in the microwave. Tip into a sieve and leave to drain well. Cook the potatoes until tender and drain well. To dry all vegetables thoroughly, drain, return to the saucepan and toss over the heat until all the moisture has evaporated.

Mash the buttercup and potato together thoroughly. Stir the beaten eggs and butter into the mixture. Mix the cheeses together and add about two-thirds to the pumpkin and potato mixture. Season with salt, a generous amount of freshly ground black pepper and the nutmeg. Butter a 1.5-litre gratin dish. Place the squash mixture in the dish and press down. Sprinkle with the remaining cheese and dribble over the 2 tablespoons of melted butter. Bake in oven until brown and bubbling, about 30 minutes.

SERVES 6

Cabbage and cumin

2 tablespoons sunflower oil
½ onion, finely sliced
1 teaspoon cumin seeds
1 kg savoy cabbage, finely shredded
1 teaspoon salt
freshly ground black pepper
5 tablespoons water

Heat oil in a pan that has a lid and fry the onion over a medium heat until soft and beginning to brown. Add the cumin seeds and cook for a further 2 minutes. Add the cabbage and toss to coat with the oil and onion. Sprinkle over salt and pepper and add water. Cover with the lid and cook briskly, tossing the pan frequently, for 5–6 minutes. Stir to mix, adjust seasoning and serve.

SERVES 4–6

Microwave cheesy vegetables

6 field mushrooms
4 stalks silverbeet
4 tomatoes
3 courgettes
1 kg potatoes, peeled and sliced
salt and freshly ground
  black pepper
4 carrots, peeled and sliced
1 onion, finely sliced
3 cloves garlic, crushed
1 tablespoon chicken
  stock powder
2 cups grated tasty cheese

Remove stalks from mushrooms and slice. Remove stalks from silverbeet and shred finely. Remove core from tomatoes and dice. Slice courgettes into thin slices. Grease a 2-litre microwave-proof casserole dish. Lay the potatoes in the bottom. Season well with salt and pepper to taste. Top with carrot slices, courgettes, mushrooms, silverbeet, diced tomatoes, onion and garlic. Sprinkle over chicken stock powder. Cover the dish tightly with plastic wrap. Place in microwave and cook for 10 minutes on High. Take from microwave and carefully remove plastic wrap. Cover the top with cheese and replace plastic wrap. Then heat again for 1 minute on High. Allow to stand for 2–3 minutes before carefully removing the plastic wrap. Serve immediately.

SERVES 4

Vegetarian dishes

Spicy squash stew

2 tablespoons olive oil
1 onion, diced
1 clove garlic, crushed
450 g potatoes, peeled and
    roughly chopped
2 tablespoons curry paste
    or powder
2½ cups liquid vegetable stock
450 g squash (butternut,
    pumpkin or buttercup),
    roughly chopped
400 g can black-eyed beans or
    kidney beans, drained
salt and freshly ground
    black pepper
2 tablespoons chopped fresh
    coriander or parsley
naan bread and lemon wedges
    to serve

In a heavy-based saucepan, heat the olive oil, then fry the onion and garlic for 3–4 minutes until softened. Add the potatoes and cook, stirring, for 3 minutes. Stir in the curry paste or powder and vegetable stock and bring to the boil. Simmer for 5 minutes, then add the squash and simmer for a further 15 minutes until the vegetables are cooked. Add the black-eyed beans and season with salt and pepper. Continue cooking until the beans are warmed through. Divide the stew among serving plates or large shallow bowls and sprinkle over the coriander or parsley. Serve with naan bread and lemon wedges.

SERVES 4

Apricot, custard and almond crumbles, page 113

Choc chip bread pudding, page 114

Desserts

A dessert is always a special way to end a meal. Portions don't need to be huge. You have just finished a large main meal, so all you need is a small sweet offering. Whether for you and your mates to enjoy while watching TV, or for when your parents come to dinner at your flat, a well-made dessert is a lovely offering to accompany coffee or a sweet dessert wine.

Use fruits that are in season and, when you can, prepare desserts that suit the season. For example, a hot crumble is great for a cold winter's night and marinated summer fruits are the perfect way to finish a meal on a balmy evening.

Desserts are like any kind of baking, measure the ingredients properly and assemble them all before you begin. If a fruit listed in the recipe is not available, it may easily be substituted with another fruit of a similar type. For example, you can use pears instead of apples or apricots instead of peaches. Any kind of berries can be swapped for another, or just be added to your favourite dessert as a yummy garnish.

Serve a dessert that suits the meal you have prepared. If you have cooked a heavy, rich main meal, it doesn't pay to accompany it with a stodgy dessert. A good dessert should cleanse the palate, not push you over the edge!

If worrying about the waistline, choose desserts made with low-fat ingredients or just choose a smaller portion. Everything in moderation.

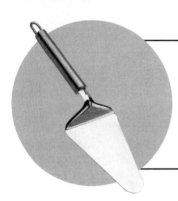

Five ways
with canned fruit

Canned fruit is a great store-cupboard food, perfect for emergency desserts and full of goodness as well.

Apricot tart
Lay 1 sheet Edmonds Flaky Puff Pastry on floured board. Cut into four. Brush with beaten egg. Lay 2–3 canned apricot halves on top of each piece of pastry. Sprinkle with raw sugar. Bake in 200°C oven for 15 minutes, until puffed and golden.

Pears and pecorino
Instead of a sweet, creamy dessert, try fruit and cheese. Perfect partners are canned pears, with chunks of a hard cheese such as pecorino or manchego. Accompany with walnuts, almonds or a bunch of grapes, and serve with a dessert wine.

Easy peach crumble
Open a can of peaches. Drain the juice and put to one side. Place peaches in the bottom of a 1-litre ovenproof dish. In a bowl, crumble 2–3 Weet-Bix with 1 cup flour, and rub in 50 g butter. Sprinkle over top of peaches. Dot with pieces of butter and cook in 180°C oven for 25 minutes. Mix the peach juice with Edmonds Custard Powder to make a peach custard.

Apple & raspberry frosty cream
Open a can of apple pieces. Drain well. Place in a freezer bag with 2 peeled and chopped bananas and 1 punnet of fresh raspberries. Place in freezer overnight to freeze. When solid, place in a food processor or blender and purée. The mixture should be creamy. Put into a plastic container and return to freezer until ready to serve.

Fruit salad dessert
In a large dessert glass, layer pieces of canned fruit salad with fruity yoghurt. Finish the top with yoghurt and sprinkle over chopped nuts. Add whipped cream and a wafer. Ice cream can be swapped for yoghurt. Top with a cherry!

Apricot, custard
and almond crumbles

825 g can apricot halves in natural juice
1 cup pre-made custard
½ cup Edmonds Self Raising Flour
¾ teaspoon ground ginger
¼ cup ground almonds
¼ cup brown sugar
¼ cup caster sugar
100 g butter, chopped

Preheat oven to 180°C. Drain the apricots over a small jug or bowl reserving ½ cup of the juice. Slice apricots and divide among six ¾-cup capacity ovenproof dishes. Place the dishes on a baking tray. Combine the custard with the reserved juice. Pour over apricots. Sift flour and ginger into a medium bowl. Stir in the almonds and sugars, then rub in butter with fingertips. Sprinkle crumble mixture over the fruit and bake in oven for about 30 minutes or until browned. Serve hot or cold with ice cream.

SERVES 6

Blueberry cheesecake

250 g packet digestive biscuits
1 teaspoon grated lemon rind
1 tablespoon lemon juice
75 g butter, melted

FILLING
200 g frozen blueberries
½ cup sugar
2 tablespoons lemon juice
1 teaspoon lemon rind
4 teaspoons gelatine
4 tablespoons water
250 g cream cheese
250 g sour cream
1 teaspoon vanilla essence

Place bisuits in a plastic bag and finely crush with a rolling pin. Combine biscuit crumbs, lemon rind, juice and butter. Line the base of a 22-cm spring-form tin with biscuit mixture. Chill while preparing filling. In a bowl, allow blueberries to thaw covered with sugar, lemon juice and rind. Combine gelatine and water. Leave to swell for 10 minutes. Beat cream cheese until soft. Add sour cream and beat until well combined. Add the vanilla. Beat in blueberry mixture, until sugar has dissolved. Beat in gelatine mixture. Stir into cheese mixture. Pour filling into prepared base. Chill until set.

SERVES 6-8

Desserts

Marinated strawberries
and passionfruit cream

1 lemon
¼ cup caster sugar
¼ cup water
1 small cinnamon stick
2 tablespoons raspberry jam
½ cup port or red wine
2 punnets strawberries, halved

PASSIONFRUIT CREAM
1½ cups cream
2 teaspoons icing sugar
2 tablespoons passionfruit pulp

Remove strips of peel from lemon using a potato peeler; place peel in a saucepan with sugar, water, cinnamon stick and jam. Stir over low heat until sugar and jam dissolve. Add port. Bring just to boiling point then remove from the heat and stand for 10 minutes. Place strawberries in a bowl and pour over the syrup. Cover and chill for 4–6 hours or overnight.

To make the passionfruit cream, whip cream until just thickened, add icing sugar and passionfruit pulp and whip till well combined. Chill before serving.

SERVES 4

Choc chip bread pudding

1 tablespoon butter, for greasing
12 slices slightly stale raisin bread or fruit loaf, cut into 2.5-cm chunks
1 cup plain chocolate chips
½ cup milk

1¼ cup cream
½ cup caster sugar
5 eggs
1 teaspoon vanilla essence
sifted cocoa powder for dusting

Place a roasting tin half-filled with water in oven and heat to 150°C. Butter a 1.4-litre shallow ovenproof dish. Remove crusts from the bread. Spread half the bread slices in bottom of dish. Sprinkle with half the chocolate chips then add the remaining bread. Stir together the milk, cream, sugar, 3 whole eggs and 2 yolks and vanilla. Whisk remaining egg whites until just stiff, then fold into cream mixture and pour over bread. Top with remaining chocolate chips and leave to stand for 30 minutes. Stand dish in preheated roasting pan, bake in oven for 40 minutes. Dust with cocoa powder and serve warm with cream.

SERVES 6

Apple shortcake

4 apples, peeled, cored and sliced
finely grated zest and juice of
½ lemon
1 tablespoon sugar
2 tablespoons water
2 cups Edmonds Standard
Grade Flour
1 teaspoon Edmonds
Baking Powder
125 g butter
¼ cup sugar
1 egg, beaten
1–2 tablespoons milk
icing sugar, to dust

Preheat oven to 180°C. Grease a 22-cm square cake tin. Put apples, lemon zest and juice, first measure of sugar and water in a saucepan and cook slowly until apples are soft. Sift flour and baking powder into a bowl. Rub in butter until it resembles coarse breadcrumbs. Mix in second measure of sugar and egg. Add sufficient milk to mix to a soft dough. Knead until smooth. Form into a ball and wrap in plastic wrap. Refrigerate for 30 minutes. Flatten half the dough in the bottom of the greased tin and spread apple over it. Lightly press remaining dough on top. Bake in oven for 25 minutes. Cool. Dust with sifted icing sugar. Cut into squares. Serve warm with ice cream.

SERVES 4–6

Baked chocolate tart

2–3 sheets Edmonds Sweet
    Short Pastry
150 g dark chocolate
60 g unsalted butter
200 ml cream
3 eggs, beaten
80 g caster sugar
1 tablespoon cocoa powder
    dissolved in 2 teaspoons
    boiling water

Preheat oven to 180°C. Grease and line a 28-cm shallow flan tin with sheets of the pastry, covering bottom and sides. Cover pastry with baking paper and spread with baking beans or rice. Place in oven and bake for 15 minutes. Remove the paper and beans or rice and cook for a further 3 minutes. Gently melt the chocolate and butter together in a bowl over a pan of boiling water. Remove chocolate from the heat, allow to cool a little and then whisk in the remaining ingredients. Pour the mixture into the cooked pastry case and bake for 25 minutes. Serve warm or cold with crème fraîche or ice cream. Decorate with a dusting of icing sugar.

SERVES 6

Lemon citron tart

SWEET SHORTCRUST PASTRY
(Makes 200 g)
1 cup Edmonds Standard Grade Flour
75 g butter
¼ cup sugar
1 egg yolk
1 tablespoon water

FILLING
4 eggs
¼ cup lemon juice
1 tablespoon grated lemon zest
½ cup caster sugar
¾ cup cream

To make the pastry, sift the flour. Rub in butter until it resembles fine breadcrumbs. Stir in sugar. Add yolk and water. Mix to a stiff dough. Cover with plastic wrap and chill for 30 minutes before using.

Preheat oven to 190°C. Roll pastry out on a lightly floured surface. Line a 20-cm round flan tin with the pastry. Refrigerate for 10 minutes. Bake blind in oven for 15 minutes. (To bake blind, cut a circle of baking paper to cover the pastry. Fill with dried beans or rice.) Remove baking blind material and cook for a further 3 minutes.

To make the filling, beat eggs, lemon juice, lemon zest and sugar until combined. Lightly beat in cream. Pour into pastry shell. Bake at 190°C for 5 minutes, then reduce temperature to 150°C and cook for a further 20–25 minutes or until tart is set. Serve warm or cold with whipped cream.

SERVES 4–6

Eaton mess, page 117

Peanut butter muesli squares, page 122

Eaton mess

150 g frozen blueberries
1 banana or a good handful raspberries
1 tablespoon caster sugar
1¼ cups cream

a few drops vanilla essence
300 ml Greek yoghurt, sweetened with honey, or plain yoghurt
6 ready-made meringues, broken into pieces

Put the blueberries into a bowl; chop and add the banana, or add the raspberries, depending on your choice. Sprinkle over the sugar and stir in. Whip the cream, together with the vanilla, until thick but not too stiff and buttery; then stir in the yoghurt. Chill the mixture for 30 minutes. Before serving, stir in the broken pieces of meringue. Eat immediately.

SERVES 4

Easy tiramisu

2 tablespoons instant coffee powder
1 cup boiling water
½ cup chocolate sauce
4 x croissants
50 g dark chocolate, grated
strawberries to decorate

FILLING
250 g cream cheese
½ cup icing sugar
1½ cups cream, whipped
⅓ cup chocolate sauce

Dissolve coffee in boiling water, stir in chocolate sauce, and allow to cool. Cut croissants into 1.5-cm thick slices. Place half the slices in a single layer over base of a deep dish. Pour over half the coffee mixture. To make the filling, beat cream cheese and icing sugar in small bowl with an electric mixer or wooden spoon until smooth. Stir in remaining ingredients and mix well. Spread half the filling over the croissants in the dish, sprinkle with half the chocolate. Place remaining croissants over filling, pour over remaining coffee mixture, top with remaining filling. Sprinkle with remaining chocolate. Cover, refrigerate for several hours or overnight. Serve decorated with strawberries.

SERVES 6-8

Desserts

Chocolate and hazelnut meringues

2 egg whites
½ cup sugar
1 teaspoon cocoa powder

50 g hazelnuts, finely chopped
whipped cream

Preheat oven to 120°C. Beat egg whites until stiff but not dry. Add half the sugar and beat well. Repeat with remaining sugar. Beat until thick and glossy. Add cocoa powder and hazelnuts. Pipe or spoon small amounts of meringue onto a greased baking tray. Bake in oven for 1–1½ hours or until the meringues are dry but not burning. Cool and, when required to serve, sandwich meringues together in pairs with whipped cream. Store unfilled meringues in an airtight container.

MAKES 12

Rhubarb and apple pie

8 stalks rhubarb
4 apples
1 cup sultanas
1 cup sugar

4 sheets Edmonds Sweet Short Pastry
50 g butter, cut into cubes
1 egg, beaten
¼ cup raw sugar

Preheat oven to 200°C. Trim leaves and stringy cords from the rhubarb stalks and wash. Cut into small pieces. Peel and remove core from apples, then dice. Place rhubarb, apple and sultanas into a heavy-based saucepan with the sugar and ½ cup water. Cook for 15 minutes, until softened. Allow to cool slightly. Grease and line a 25-cm flan tin with 2 pastry sheets, leaving a flap of pastry on the sides. Spoon the rhubarb and apple over the pastry. Sprinkle over the butter cubes. Top with the remaining sheets of pastry. Trim and fold up the edges, sealing them well. Cut 2 or 3 slits in the middle to allow heat to escape. Brush top of pie with beaten egg and sprinkle over the raw sugar. Bake in oven for 30 minutes until pastry is golden brown.

SERVES 6

Pear tarte tatin

820 g can pear halves
50 g butter
1 cup sugar

2 sheets Edmonds Flaky
Puff Pastry

Preheat oven to 220°C. Drain pears. Melt butter and sugar in a frying pan about 20 cm in diameter and with a metal handle. Arrange pears in a cartwheel fashion in the pan. Brush one pastry sheet lightly with water and place second sheet on top of first. Cut pastry to the same diameter as the frying pan used. Place pastry over pears and cook over a medium heat for 15 minutes. Remove from heat and place pan in oven. Bake in oven for 10–15 minutes or until pastry is golden. Turn onto a serving plate and serve hot.

SERVES 4–6

Banana rice pudding

1 tablespoon butter
½ cup short-grain rice
½ cup dried bananas, chopped into small pieces
2 cups milk

1½ cups cream
1½ tablespoons runny honey
few drops vanilla essence
½ teaspoon grated nutmeg

Preheat oven to 150°C. Butter a 850-ml ovenproof dish. Pour in the remaining ingredients and stir until the honey has dissolved. Bake in the middle of the oven for 1¾–2 hours.

SERVES 4

Desserts

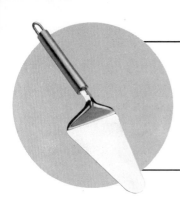

How to make ice cream

Making your own ice cream seems redundant when there are many brands out there doing just nicely thank you. But it holds the same reward as baking a loaf of bread or cooking your own burgers. You can control the input of additives, there is no need for preservatives and you can experiment with many different flavours.

Simple vanilla ice cream

4 eggs, separated
¼ cup caster sugar
¼ cup caster sugar

1 teaspoon vanilla essence
1½ cups cream

Beat egg whites until stiff peaks form. Gradually add first measure of sugar, 1 tablespoon at a time, beating until sugar dissolves before adding the next tablespoon. In a separate bowl beat egg yolks and second measure of sugar until thick and pale. Add vanilla. Gently fold in yolk mixture. In another bowl beat cream until thick then fold into egg mixture. Pour mixture into a shallow container suitable for freezing. Freeze for 2 hours or until firm. Use a fork to turn the mixture over and then re-freeze. For a great ice cream, repeat this process 3–4 times.

VARIATIONS
Any of the following can be added after the cream: 1 cup chocolate chips, 1 cup chopped nuts, 1 cup puréed berries, e.g. strawberries, raspberries.

Hints
- For the creamiest texture make and chill the ice cream mixture the day before you plan to use it.
- If using an ice cream maker fill only two-thirds full as the mixture expands as it freezes.
- A freshly frozen mixture thaws quickly, so don't handle it too much or leave it out of the freezer unnecessarily.
- Avoid making lumpy ice cream by not having a warm mixture. Make sure the mixture is room temperature before freezing.
- Don't store the ice cream for too long – it will just turn into ice crystals and lose all its flavour. Home-made ice cream is best eaten 'fresh'.

Cakes and baking

Make a cake or bake a batch of biscuits and really impress your flatmates. Always remember to read the recipe properly and make sure you set out all the ingredients before you start.

All weights and measures are given from using standard equipment. One cup is a standard 250 ml measurement. Try to invest in a set of measuring cups and spoons; this will ensure your measurements are correct. For any baking recipe, put flour or sugar into a measuring cup then level off the top with the back of a knife. If using brown sugar, pack it into the cup to get the correct measurement. Here are a few simple guidelines for making cakes and biscuits:

Cakes
- Make sure the eggs are at room temperature. Leave chilled eggs in warm water for 5 minutes, if necessary, before you start baking.
- Cream butter and sugar until light and fluffy. This usually means that the sugar is dissolved and the mixture looks almost like overwhipped cream.
- Grease and line the tin with baking paper. Cut out a circle or square to fit the bottom of the tin, then thin strips of paper to cover the sides. Grease the bottom and sides of the tin to help the paper stick to it.

Biscuits
- Avoid using too much flour, or overmixing the dough as this will make the biscuits hard and tough.
- For even baking, shape biscuits to the same thickness and roll out a small amount of biscuit dough at a time. Keep remainder of the dough covered with plastic wrap to keep it moist.

Enjoy the baking process! Take your time and think about what you are doing and the results will follow. Invite some friends around to share in the process and then the products of your endeavours can be enjoyed, together, straight out of the oven.

No-bake chocolate cake

275 g plain chocolate
175 g butter
4 tablespoons golden syrup
2 tablespoons dark rum (optional)
175 g plain biscuits, e.g. round wine
1 cup rice bubbles
50 g chopped pecan nuts
100 g roughly chopped glacé cherries
25 g white chocolate buttons

Melt together the plain chocolate, butter, golden syrup and rum, if using. Roughly break up the biscuits into small pieces and toss with the rice bubbles, nuts and cherries. Pour the chocolate mixture over the crushed biscuits, fruit and nuts. Line a 20-cm square cake tin with plastic wrap. Spoon the chocolate mixture into the lined tin. Press down well with the back of a spoon then chill for 2 hours. To decorate, melt the white chocolate and drizzle randomly over the top. Allow to harden. To serve, carefully turn out of tin, pull away the plastic wrap and cut into 16 squares. Store in an airtight container in the fridge for up to 2 weeks.

Variation: Brandy or Grand Marnier can also be used instead of rum, or try adding 25 g desiccated coconut instead of the rice bubbles and using a coconut rum liqueur such as Malibu.

MAKES 16 PIECES

Peanut butter muesli squares

½ cup desiccated coconut
375 g can sweetened condensed milk
3 cups toasted muesli
¼ cup runny honey
¼ cup smooth peanut butter
50 g butter, chopped into cubes
½ cup unsalted roasted peanuts
1 cup icing sugar

Grease a 20-cm x 30-cm sponge roll tin and line base and long sides with non-stick baking paper, extending paper 2 cm over top of tin. Spread half of coconut over base of prepared tin. Combine remaining ingredients in a large saucepan and stir on low heat for 15 minutes, until mixture is thick. Spread mixture over coconut in tin. Sprinkle with remaining coconut, pressing down gently. Cover and chill for 1–2 hours, until firm. Slice into squares and serve.

MAKES 30 PIECES

Feijoa and pecan cake, page 123

Basic loaf of bread, page 130

Feijoa and pecan cake

250 g butter, softened
1½ cups sugar
4 eggs
3 cups mashed ripe feijoas
2 teaspoon Edmonds Baking Soda
4 tablespoons hot milk
4 cups Edmonds Standard Grade Flour
2 teaspoons Edmonds Baking Powder
½ teaspoon cinnamon
50 g pecan nuts, roughly chopped
extra pecan nuts, to decorate

LEMON CREAM CHEESE ICING
2 tablespoons butter, softened
¼ cup cream cheese
1 cup icing sugar
½ teaspoon lemon zest

Preheat oven to 180°C. Cream butter and sugar until light and fluffy. Add eggs, one at a time, beating well after each addition. Add mashed feijoa and mix thoroughly. Stir soda into hot milk and add to creamed mixture. Sift flour, baking powder and cinnamon. Fold into mixture with pecan nuts. Turn into a greased and lined 22-cm round cake tin. Bake in oven for 50 minutes or until cake springs back when lightly touched. Leave in tin for 10 minutes before turning out onto a wire rack. When cold, ice with Lemon Cream Cheese Icing and garnish with chopped pecan nuts.

To make the icing, beat butter and cream cheese until creamy. Mix in icing sugar and lemon rind, beating well to combine.

Banana and mango cake

125 g butter, softened
½ cup brown sugar, firmly packed
2 eggs
3 ripe bananas, mashed
½ x 400 g can mango slices, drained
1½ cups Edmonds Self Raising Flour
1 teaspoon Edmonds Baking Soda
¾ cup sour cream
1 tablespoon milk

LEMON AND MANGO ICING
60 g cream cheese
25 g butter
1 teaspoon grated lemon rind
1 tablespoon lemon juice
2 cups icing sugar
½ x 400 g can mango slices, drained

Lightly grease a deep 23-cm round cake tin. Preheat oven to 180°C. Cream butter and sugar in a large bowl with electric mixer until light and fluffy. Add eggs, one at a time, beating after each addition, until well combined. Stir in banana and mango, then stir in sifted dry ingredients and combined sour cream and milk in 2 batches. Pour mixture into prepared tin, bake in oven for about 1 hour, or until cake springs back when touched. Stand in tin for 5 minutes. Turn onto wire rack to cool. Spread cold banana cake with Lemon and Mango Icing. To make the icing, beat cream cheese, butter, rind, juice and mango slices in a small bowl with electric mixer until light and fluffy. Gradually add sifted icing sugar, beat until smooth.

Bran muffins

2 cups Edmonds Standard Grade Flour
2 teaspoons Edmonds Baking Powder
1 teaspoon salt
1 teaspoon mixed spice
3 cups Edmonds Wheat Bran
½ cup brown sugar
2 eggs
2 teaspoons Edmonds Baking Soda
2 cups milk
2 tablespoons golden syrup
50 g butter
1 cup sultanas

Preheat oven to 220°C. Sift flour, baking powder, salt and mixed spice into a large bowl. Mix in bran and brown sugar. Lightly beat eggs. Dissolve baking soda in milk. Melt golden syrup and butter together. Make a well in the centre of the dry ingredients. Add eggs, milk mixture, melted ingredients and sultanas. Mix quickly until just combined. Bake in oven for 15 minutes or until muffins spring back when lightly touched.

MAKES 12

Date flapjack

2 cups dates, chopped
1 cup boiling water
250 g butter
2 teaspoons vanilla essence
4 cups rolled oats
1 cup Champion Standard Grade Flour
1½ cups brown sugar

Preheat oven to 180°C. Grease and line a sponge roll tin with baking paper. Soak the dates in the boiling water for 20–30 minutes. Melt butter in a saucepan, then stir in the vanilla, oats, flour and brown sugar. Press half the mixture into tin and top with dates. Place the remaining oat mixture on top. Press down firmly. Bake in oven for 30 minutes. Allow to cool before cutting into squares.

MAKES 16 PIECES

Cakes and baking

Hummingbird cake

1 cup Edmonds Standard Grade Flour
½ cup Edmonds Self Raising Flour
½ teaspoon Edmonds Baking Soda
½ teaspoon ground cinnamon
½ teaspoon ground ginger
1 cup brown sugar
½ cup desiccated coconut
2 eggs, beaten lightly
¾ cup extra light olive oil
1 cup mashed banana
450 g can crushed pineapple in syrup, drained

PASSIONFRUIT ICING
90 g cream cheese
100 g butter, softened
1 cup icing sugar
1 tablespoon passionfruit pulp

Preheat oven to 180°C. Grease a deep, 19-cm square cake tin and line the base with baking paper. Sift the flours, baking soda and spices into a large bowl then stir in the sugar and coconut. Add the combined eggs and oil, then the banana and pineapple. Mix well. Spread the mixture into the prepared tin and bake in oven for about 1 hour. Stand the cake in the tin for 5 minutes before turning onto a wire rack to cool. Top the cold cake with Passionfruit Icing.

To make Passionfruit Icing, beat the cream cheese and butter in a small bowl with a wooden spoon or an electric beater. Gradually beat in sifted icing sugar, then stir in the passionfruit pulp.

Muesli biscuits

2½ cups Edmonds Standard
   Grade Flour
1 cup brown sugar
2 cups desiccated coconut
1½ cups rolled oats
1 cup currants
½ cup pumpkin seeds
½ cup sunflower seeds
400 g butter
6 tablespoons golden syrup
2 teaspoons Edmonds
   Baking Soda
¾ cup boiling water
1 teaspoon vanilla essence

In a large bowl, mix together flour, sugar, coconut, rolled oats, currants, pumpkin seeds and sunflower seeds. In a small saucepan, melt butter and golden syrup. Dissolve baking soda in the boiling water and add to butter and golden syrup. Add vanilla essence. Stir butter mixture into the dry ingredients. Place level tablespoonfuls of mixture onto cold greased baking trays and press down lightly with a fork. Bake at 180°C for about 15 minutes or until golden.

MAKES 30

Louise cake

150 g butter, softened
¼ cup sugar
4 eggs, separated
2 cups Champion Standard
   Grade Flour
2 teaspoons Edmonds
   Baking Powder
¼ cup raspberry jam
½ cup caster sugar
½ cup coconut

Cream butter and sugar until light and fluffy. Beat in egg yolks. Sift flour and baking powder together. Stir into creamed mixture. Press dough into a greased 20 cm x 30 cm sponge-roll tin lined on the base with baking paper. Spread raspberry jam over the base.

Using an electric mixer, beat egg whites until soft peaks form. Gradually add caster sugar, beating continuously. Beat until glossy. Fold in coconut. Spread meringue mixture over jam. Bake at 180°C for 30 minutes or until meringue is dry and lightly coloured. Cut into squares while still warm.

MAKES 12 SLICES

Lemon sour cream cake

125 g butter, softened
2 teaspoons grated lemon rind
1 cup sugar
3 eggs
1 cup Champion Standard Grade Flour
1 teaspoon Edmonds Baking Powder
½ cup sour cream
icing sugar

Preheat oven to 160°C. Beat butter, lemon rind, sugar and eggs together until light and fluffy. Sift flour and baking powder together. Fold sifted ingredients into egg mixture alternately with sour cream, mixing until smooth. Pour mixture into a greased and lined 20-cm round cake tin. Bake in oven for 45 minutes or until the cake springs back when lightly touched. Leave in tin for 5–10 minutes before turning out onto a wire rack. When cold, dust with icing sugar.

Shortbread

250 g butter, softened
1 cup icing sugar
1 cup Edmonds Fielder's Cornflour
2 cups Edmonds Standard Grade Flour

Preheat oven to 180°C. Cream butter and icing sugar until light and fluffy. Sift cornflour and flour together. Mix sifted ingredients into creamed mixture. Knead well. Divide dough into two equal portions and form into logs, about 6 cm across and 2 cm deep. Cover with plastic wrap and refrigerate for 1 hour. Cut into 1-cm thick slices. Place on greased baking trays. Prick with a fork. Bake in oven for 15–20 minutes or until a pale golden colour.

MAKES ABOUT 35

Ham, mustard and cheese muffins

1 tablespoon wholegrain mustard
100 g ham, chopped
¾ cup grated tasty cheese
2 cups Champion Standard
    Grade Flour
pinch cayenne pepper
4 teaspoons Edmonds
    Baking Powder
¼ teaspoon salt
1 egg, beaten
50 g butter, melted
½ cup milk

Put mustard, ham and cheese into a bowl. Sift flour, cayenne pepper, baking powder and salt into the bowl. Stir to combine. Quickly stir in egg, butter and milk just to moisten. Spoon mixture into greased muffin tins. Bake at 200°C for 15 minutes or until golden.

Wholemeal yoghurt scones

1 cup Edmonds Wholemeal Flour
1 cup Edmonds Standard
    Grade Flour
1 teaspoon Edmonds Baking Soda
3 teaspoons Edmonds
    Baking Powder
50 g butter
1 teaspoon sugar
½ cup fruit yoghurt
¼–½ cup milk
extra milk

Preheat oven to 220°C. Sift wholemeal flour, flour, soda and baking powder into a bowl. (If any husks are left in the sifter, add them to the bowl.) Rub butter into flour mixture until it resembles breadcrumbs. Stir in sugar and yoghurt. Add sufficient milk to mix to a soft dough. Lightly dust a baking tray with flour. Press scone dough out to a 20-cm round and mark into eight wedges. Brush top with milk. Bake in oven for 10 minutes or until pale golden.

How to
make a basic loaf of bread

It takes 3–4 hours to make a loaf of bread, but most of that time is spent waiting for nature. That seems like a long time, but once you try it and realise how much fun it is and how good it tastes, you'll enjoy the experience! And the possibilities are endless. Wow your friends and family with a loaf, plait or rolls made with your own hands and your selection of flavourings. It's not hard; you can control what ingredients go into your bread; it's cheaper than most shop-bought bread and way more satisfying. Follow these easy steps . . .

To make 2 x 900 g loaves:

2 teaspoons Edmonds Surebake Yeast
25 g butter, at room temperature
2 teaspoons sugar
2 teaspoons salt
700 g Edmonds High Grade Flour, plus extra for kneading
1 medium egg yolk
2 tablespoons cream
poppy seeds or sesame seeds for topping
salt

Prepare 2 x 900 g loaf tins (standard loaf tins) by brushing them well with oil.

Step one
In a small bowl, mix the yeast with 150 ml lukewarm water and stir until dissolved. Place the butter, sugar and salt in another bowl, along with 150 ml of very hot water, and stir until the sugar and salt have completely dissolved and the butter has melted. Add 150 ml of cold water to the butter mixture – the liquid should be lukewarm – then stir in the dissolved yeast.

Step two
Sieve the flour into a large bowl, then make a well in the centre and pour in almost all the liquid. Mix to a loose dough, first using a wooden spoon and then your hands, adding the remainder of the liquid if to dry. Turn the dough out onto a floured board, cover it with a clean tea towel and leave to relax for 5–10 minutes.

Step three
Knead the dough for about 10 minutes, or until smooth and springy (if using a food mixer with a dough hook, 5 minutes is usually long enough). The purpose of kneading is to develop the gluten in the dough – the more one kneads, the more elastic the dough becomes, giving the bread a better texture. To check whether the dough has been kneaded enough, push it with your finger – it should immediately spring back. Place the dough in a clean ceramic bowl and cover tightly with plastic wrap. Dough rises best in a warm, moist atmosphere, such as near the oven or on top of the oven with the heat turned onto low (or the hot-water cupboard is good too). The time it takes to rise will depend on the temperature, but it will probably need about 1 hour.

Step four
When the dough has doubled in size, turn it out onto a lightly floured surface and knead it again for 2–3 minutes, until all the air has been forced out again – this is called 'knocking back'. Cover the dough with a clean tea towel and leave it to relax again for a further 10 minutes or so. Now divide the dough in two, place the pieces in the tins and cover with the tea towel. If you prefer, you can make a plait or smaller rolls.

Step five
Leave the dough to rise again in a warm place for about 30 minutes. Meanwhile, preheat oven to 230°C. The dough is ready for baking if, when pressed lightly, a small dent remains – the dough should not spring back. Mix together the egg yolk and cream, then gently brush the loaves with the mixture and sprinkle with the poppy or sesame seeds, if using. Bake on the middle shelf of the oven for 30–35 minutes, until the bread is golden brown and the loaves sound hollow when tipped out of the tins and tapped on the bottom.

Different toppings for loaves
Oatmeal, kibbled wheat, pumpkin seeds or sunflower seeds.

party food

Having a party is fun – a few drinks, some good music and a few good laughs. Don't forget your host responsibility: serve some food. Snacks and finger food are best served with beers, wines and spirits to help the absorption of alcohol, not to mention the enjoyment of the food and wine combinations!

Plan ahead as much as possible. You can make some things ahead of time, so the foods can be put together on the day very easily. Remember to refrigerate any prepared foods. Make only 1 or 2 finger foods which require last-minute preparation, and serve some that require no cooking at all, such as cheese, nuts and grapes or assorted salamis. For maximum flavour, remove cold foods from the fridge about 30 minutes before serving.

How much is enough? Allow 10–12 portions of food per guest if no meal is being served. Otherwise, allow 4–5 portions per guest. Present food well; for example, take notice of the colours of food you are combining on a plate. Use colourful plates to complement the different foods that are going on them. Don't be scared to experiment with different platters. There is no need to stick to white.

Which wine to serve? The million-dollar question! In a party full of people with different tastes, there is no need to have lots of different bottles, unless every guest brings their own bottle. If you are supplying the wine, then choose one that is your favourite, something you know and enjoy. Talking about that wine is a perfect way to break the ice with your guests. Read the label and feel empowered with knowledge!

A great way to decide on the food and drink you are serving is to establish a theme. How about the beginning of a new season, a country's cuisine, or just a simple, fun theme like a movie title. A theme can help with decoration around your flat or rented house.

Most importantly, relax and enjoy yourself. Your guests are there for a good time and to enjoy your company, not to watch you get into a flap over burnt sausage rolls!

Spring vegetables in rice wrappers, page 133

Smoked salmon and goats' cheese roll-ups, page 134

Spring vegetables
in rice wrappers

CHILLI DIPPING SAUCE
¼ cup rice wine vinegar
1 tablespoon sweet chilli sauce
1 tablespoon brown sugar
1 teaspoon grated root ginger

VEGETABLE RICE WRAPPERS
2 carrots, peeled
1 telegraph cucumber
1 yellow capsicum
1 red capsicum
250 g mung bean sprouts
2 spring onions, finely sliced
2 tablespoons sweet chilli sauce
1 tablespoon soy sauce
24 Vietnamese rice wrappers (dried)

To make the dipping sauce, combine all ingredients. Mix well. To make the fresh rice wrappers, slice the carrots thinly into 5-cm strips. Cut the cucumber into thin 5-cm strips. De-seed and remove pith from the capsicums and slice thinly into small strips. Mix the carrots, cucumber, capsicums, bean sprouts and spring onions together in a bowl. Add the sweet chilli and soy sauce and toss through. Take one rice wrapper at a time. Dip in cold water until softened. Place a spoonful of the vegetable mixture in the middle. Fold edges in and roll up to enclose. Place on a tray in the refrigerator until ready to serve. Cut in half and serve with the Chilli Dipping Sauce.

MAKES 24

Party food

Smoked salmon
and goat's cheese roll-ups

200 g goat's cheese or feta cheese
150 g cream cheese, softened
2 tablespoons capers, roughly chopped
2 tablespoons lemon juice
salt and freshly ground black pepper
12 smoked salmon slices
½ cup ready-made pesto

In a large bowl, place the crumbled goat's cheese, cream cheese and capers. Add lemon juice and season with salt and pepper to taste. Remove the smoked salmon slices from between the plastic leaves. Cut in half. Place a small spoonful of the cheese mixture in the middle of each piece of salmon. Roll the salmon up encasing the cheese mixture. Place on a platter and keep refrigerated until ready to serve. Serve with pesto.

MAKES 24

Prawn toasts

225 g finely chopped prawns
2 spring onions, finely chopped
2 teaspoons dry sherry
1 teaspoon grated root ginger
1 egg white
2 teaspoons Edmonds Fielder's Cornflour
8 slices white bread, crusts removed
½ cup sesame seeds
oil for shallow frying

Mix together the prawns, spring onions, sherry, ginger, egg white and cornflour. Spread onto the white bread, and sprinkle with sesame seeds. Shallow fry for 1–2 minutes, turning once, until golden.

SERVES 4

Thai chicken meatballs
with satay sauce

500 g chicken mince
2 tablespoons sweet chilli sauce
1 teaspoon ground cumin
1 cup fresh breadcrumbs
2 tablespoons fresh
    chopped parsley
pinch cayenne pepper
2 spring onions, finely chopped
1 red capsicum, finely sliced
salt and freshly ground
    black pepper

SATAY SAUCE
2 tablespoons oil
1 clove garlic, crushed
1 onion, chopped
¼–½ teaspoon chilli powder
½ cup crunchy peanut butter
1 tablespoon soy sauce
1 tablespoon lemon juice
1 tablespoon brown sugar
¾ cup coconut cream
salt

Preheat oven to 200°C. Place all ingredients in a large bowl and mix well. Roll spoonfuls into small balls. Place on a baking tray lined with foil. Cook in oven for 15 minutes, until meatballs start to turn golden. Serve warm with Satay Sauce.

SATAY SAUCE
Heat oil in a saucepan. Add garlic, onion and chilli powder. Cook until onion is clear. Stir in peanut butter, soy sauce, lemon juice and sugar. Add coconut cream. Cook until mixture boils, stirring constantly. Season with salt to taste. Add more sugar if necessary. Makes 1¼ cups.

Chicken liver pâté
with melba toast

500 g chicken livers
50 g butter
1 small onion, finely chopped
2 cloves garlic, crushed
sprig thyme
100 g butter, softened
2 tablespoons brandy
salt and freshly ground
　　black pepper
clarified butter, to coat
1 bay leaf

MELBA TOAST
6 slices white bread
extra oil or clarified butter

Trim fat and membrane from livers. Set aside. Heat first measure of butter in a frying pan. Add onion and garlic and cook until onion is clear. Remove from pan and set aside. Add chicken livers to pan and quickly cook for 5 minutes or until livers are browned but still a little pink in centre. Put onion mixture and livers into the bowl of a food processor or blender. Process until finely chopped. Add thyme, second measure of butter, brandy and salt and pepper to taste. Process to combine. Spoon mixture into a serving dish, smoothing over the top surface. Melt clarified butter. Pour this over pâté. Set bay leaf on top. Allow to cool. Cover and chill overnight.

To make the melba toast, cut the crusts of bread slices, then cut the bread into triangles. Brush with oil or clarified butter and lay on a baking tray. Bake in oven for 8 minutes, until golden brown. Serve warm with fresh pâté.

MAKES ABOUT 2 CUPS

Falafels with yoghurt sauce

YOGHURT SAUCE
1 cup natural unsweetened yoghurt
1 clove garlic, crushed
1 tablespoon chopped fresh parsley
1 tablespoon tahini
¼ teaspoon ground cumin
freshly ground black pepper to season

FALAFEL
2 x 300 g cans chickpeas in brine
1 stalk celery, chopped
1 onion, diced
1 clove garlic, crushed
2 tablespoons Champion Standard Grade Flour
2 tablespoons tahini
1 teaspoon ground cumin
½ teaspoon turmeric
salt and freshly ground black pepper
Champion Standard Grade Flour to coat
vegetable oil to cook

To make the yoghurt sauce, combine all ingredients. Mix well. Cover and refrigerate until required. To make the falafels, place chickpeas, celery, onion, garlic, flour, tahini, cumin, turmeric, salt and pepper in a food processor. Blend to a coarse consistency. Transfer to a bowl. Cover and refrigerate for 1 hour. Spread a little flour onto a flat plate. Take large teaspoonfuls of mixture and roll into balls, then flatten slightly with the palm of the hand to make a little patty. Roll in flour to lightly coat. Pour oil into a frying pan to a depth of 1 cm. Heat pan. Cook falafels for about 5 minutes, or until golden, turning once. Drain on absorbent paper. Serve with Yoghurt Sauce.

MAKES 36

Devils on horseback

8 well-soaked or ready-to-eat prunes
12 rashers rindless streaky bacon

Preheat oven to 200°C. Remove stones from prunes. Cut each rasher of bacon in half. Wrap each prune in bacon. Secure with a toothpick. Place on a baking tray. Bake in oven until bacon is cooked, turning once or twice. Serve warm.

MAKES 24

Thai fish cakes

185 g can tuna in brine
1 teaspoon ground coriander
1 teaspoon Thai fish sauce
¼ cup coconut cream
1 egg

2 tablespoons chopped
  fresh coriander
1 teaspoon prepared minced chilli
1½ cups soft breadcrumbs
½ teaspoon salt
¼ cup peanut oil

Drain tuna. Place tuna, coriander, fish sauce, coconut cream, egg, fresh coriander, chilli, breadcrumbs and salt in a food processor. Process until just combined but not paste-like. Drop tablespoonfuls of mixture into hot oil in a frying pan and cook until golden on both sides. Drain on absorbent paper and serve hot.

MAKES 26

Bacon-wrapped bananas

MAKES 8

2 bananas
lemon juice
4 rashers rindless streaky bacon

Peel bananas and cut each into 4 pieces. Brush with lemon juice. Cut each rasher of bacon in half. Wrap bananas in bacon. Secure with toothpicks. Grill on both sides until bacon is cooked. Serve warm.

MAKES 8

Mixed satays

350 g piece fast-fry steak, e.g. rump, porterhouse, fillet
2 boneless chicken breasts, skin removed
18 shelled raw king prawns
18 x 20-cm long wooden skewers

MARINADE
¾ cup coconut milk
3 tablespoons soy sauce
3 tablespoons vegetable oil
3 cloves garlic, crushed
1 teaspoon ground cumin
1 teaspoon ground coriander

Remove any visible fat from the steak and chicken. Cut lengthwise into thin strips. Place beef, chicken, and prawns in individual bowls. Make marinade by combining all ingredients. Divide marinade between the 3 bowls. Cover and refrigerate for 1–2 hours. Soak skewers in cold water for 30 minutes to prevent burning while cooking. Thread beef onto 6 skewers and chicken onto 6 skewers. Thread 3 prawns onto each of the remaining 6 skewers. Place beef and chicken skewers in a single layer on a baking tray. Preheat oven grill. Grill for 6–8 minutes, turning occasionally, then add prawn skewers and cook for a further 4–6 minutes until cooked through. Serve with Peanut Dip (page 29).

MAKES 18

Salmon puffs

1 sheet Edmonds Flaky Puff Pastry
1 egg yolk
1 tablespoon water
½ cup cream cheese

¼ cup cream, whipped
100 g smoked salmon, chopped
1 tablespoon lemon juice
1 tablespoon chopped parsley
freshly ground black pepper

Cut out rounds from the pastry, about 5 cm in diameter. Place pastry rounds onto an oven tray and prick all over with a fork. Combine egg yolk and water in a bowl. Brush pastry rounds with egg mixture. Bake at 200°C for 8–10 minutes until puffed up. Spilt rounds apart and allow to cool. Beat together cream cheese, cream, salmon, lemon juice, parsley and pepper to taste. Spread salmon mixture onto bottom rounds. Replace pastry tops.

MAKES ABOUT 20

Mini risotto balls

2 tablespoons olive oil
1 onion, very finely chopped
2 cloves garlic, crushed
2 cups arborio rice
5 cups heated liquid chicken stock or boiling water
50 g butter
2 tablespoons basil leaves
100 g parmesan cheese, grated
1 cup Champion Standard Grade Flour
3 eggs, beaten with 2 tablespoons milk
2 cups dry breadcrumbs
oil for frying

Heat oil in a large saucepan. Add onion and garlic and cook until clear. Add the rice and stir until well coated in oil. Add the stock or water 1 cup at a time. Stir and allow to cook for 5 minutes between each addition, allowing 20 minutes in total cooking time. Remove pan from heat. Add the butter and leave to melt. Slice basil. Mix basil and parmesan into risotto mixture. Allow mixture to cool. Shape, using clean hands, into about 36 walnut-sized balls. Roll each ball in flour, dip in egg and roll in breadcrumbs. Chill. Heat the oil to 190°C or until a cube of bread turns golden brown in 40 seconds. Cook risotto balls in oil until golden brown. Drain on kitchen paper.

MAKES ABOUT 36

Brandy balls

250 g packet vanilla wine biscuits
2 tablespoons currants
2 tablespoons chopped walnuts
1 egg
¼ cup sugar
1 tablespoon cocoa
1½ tablespoons brandy or sherry
125 g butter, melted
coconut or chocolate hail

Place biscuits in a plastic bag and finely crush with a rolling pin. Combine biscuit crumbs, currants and walnuts in a bowl. In another bowl, lightly beat the egg with a fork. Add sugar and cocoa, stirring until thoroughly mixed. Add brandy. Pour into crumb mixture and shape into balls. Roll in coconut or chocolate hail. Chill until firm.

MAKES ABOUT 26

Index

Aioli 30
apples
    Apple and raspberry frosty cream 112
    Apple shortcake 115
    Rhubarb and apple pie 118
apricots
    Apricot, custard and almond crumbles 113
    Apricot tart 112
    Chicken and apricot salad 42
    Lemon and apricot chicken 86
    Pork, apricot and ginger skewers 83
avocados
    Quick nachos 31
    Tomato and avocado salsa bruschetta 23
    Tostadas 34

bacon
    Bacon and egg pie 34
    Bacon-wrapped bananas 138
    Boston baked beans 82
    Creamy mushrooms and bacon 21
    Devils on horseback 137
    Fettucine with bacon, mushrooms and blue cheese 55
    Liver and bacon 83
    Pea and bacon risotto 54
    Pea and ham soup 49
    Potato bacon frittata 81
baked beans
    Boston baked beans 82
    Spicy baked beans 24
bananas
    Bacon-wrapped bananas 138
    Banana and mango cake 124
    Banana caramel pancakes 21
    Banana rice pudding 119
    Chocolate and banana porridge 19
    Eaton mess 117
beans, dried – see also baked beans
    Bean and garlic dip 30
    Quick nachos 31
    Spicy squash stew 110
    Tostadas 34
beans, green: One pot savoury beans and rice 55
beef
    Beef and vegetable casserole 68
    Beef stroganoff 69
    Corned beef with mustard sauce 67
    Mixed satays 139
    Oxtail stew 70
    Roast beef with Yorkshire pudding 66
    Spaghetti and meatballs 59
    Spicy beef and noodle stir-fry 65
    Steak and mushroom potato top pie 64
    Steak, how to cook 71–2
    Thai red beef curry 69
Beetroot and chickpea salad 41
biscuits and slices 121
    Brandy balls 140
    Date flapjack 125

Louise cake 127
Muesli biscuits 127
Peanut butter muesli squares 122
Shortbread 128
Blackened chicken 87
blueberries
    Blueberry cheesecake 113
    Eaton mess 117
Boston baked beans 82
Bran muffins 125
Brandy balls 140
Bread 130–1
Bruschetta, tomato and avocado salsa 23
Buttermilk hotcakes 24

Cabbage and cumin 108
Caesar salad dressing 38
Caesar salad, grilled chicken 45
cakes 121
    Banana and mango cake 124
    Feijoa and pecan cake 123
    Hummingbird cake 126
    Lemon sour cream cake 128
    No-bake chocolate cake 122
Calzone 33
Carrot and lentil soup, spicy 50
cheese
    Calzone 33
    Cheese tomato and bread pudding 106
    Courgette and cottage cheese fritters 22
    Fettucine with bacon, mushrooms and blue cheese 55
    Ham and mozzarella cannelloni 56
    Ham, mustard and cheese muffins 129
    Italian sandwiches 32
    Microwave cheesy vegetables 109
    Minted peas with yoghurt and feta 102
    Parmesan crumbed chicken 88
    Pears and pecorino 112
    Quick nachos 31
    Silverbeet and feta pie 107
    Silverbeet, orange and haloumi salad 40
    Smoked salmon and goat's cheese roll-ups 134
    Spinach, herb and feta frittatas (gluten free) 23
    Tomato, olive and cottage cheese dip 29
    Vegetable and cottage cheese lasagna 103
Cheesecake, blueberry 113
chicken 92
    Blackened chicken 87
    Chicken and apricot salad 42
    Chicken and mushroom egg noodles 28
    Chicken and mushroom pie 89
    Chicken liver pâté with melba toast 136
    Citrus and balsamic-glazed chicken 87
    Grilled chicken caesar salad 45
    Indian butter chicken 86
    Lemon and apricot chicken 86
    Mixed satays 139
    Mustard chicken loaf 85
    Parmesan crumbed chicken 88

Pumpkin and chicken filo pies 90
Pumpkin and smoked chicken risotto 58
Roast chicken 91–2
Spanish paella 95
Tandoori chicken drumsticks 88
Thai chicken curry 90
Thai chicken meatballs with satay sauce 135
Tostadas 34
chickpeas
    Chickpea and beetroot salad 41
    Felafels with yoghurt sauce 137
chocolate
    Baked chocolate tart 115
    Choc chip bread pudding 114
    Chocolate and banana porridge 19
    Chocolate and hazelnut meringues 118
    Easy tiramisu 117
    No-bake chocolate cake 122
Citrus and balsamic-glazed chicken 87
corn
    Creamy corn chowder 49
    Wheat-free corn fritters 22
Corned beef with mustard sauce 67
courgettes
    Courgette and cottage cheese fritters 22
    One pot savoury beans and rice 55
Couscous and salami 63
curries
    Sweet potato vegetable curry 104
    Thai chicken curry 90
    Thai red beef curry 69

Date flapjack 125
desserts – see also cakes
    Apple shortcake 115
    Apricot tart 112
    Apricot, custard and almond crumbles 113
    Baked chocolate tart 115
    Banana rice pudding 119
    Blueberry cheesecake 113
    Choc chip bread pudding 114
    Chocolate and hazelnut meringues 118
    Easy tiramisu 117
    Eaton mess 117
    Five ways with canned fruit 112
    Ice cream 120
    Lemon citron tart 116
    Marinated strawberries and
        passionfruit cream 114
    Pear tarte tatin 119
    Rhubarb and apple pie 118
Devils on horseback 137
dips
    Bean and garlic dip 30
    Chilli dipping sauce 133
    Peanut dip 29
    Sour cream and relish dip 29
    Tomato, olive and cottage cheese dip 29
dressings
    Basic vinaigrette 37
    Caesar salad dressing 38
    Honey and mustard salad dressing 37
    Lime and chilli salad dressing 37
    Soy and sesame salad dressing 37
    Yoghurt dressing 41

egg noodles – see noodles
eggs
    Bacon and egg pie 34
    Boiled eggs 25

Cheese tomato and bread pudding 106
Fried eggs 26
Poached eggs 25
Potato bacon frittata 81
Scrambled eggs 26
Spinach, herb and feta frittatas (gluten free) 23

Feijoa and pecan cake 123
Felafels with yoghurt sauce 137
Fettucine with bacon, mushrooms
    and blue cheese 55
fish 99–100 – see also salmon
    Crunchy-topped fish fillets 98
    Easy seafood chowder 48
    Egg noodle and tuna nest 28
    Fish and smoked mussel pie 98
    Fish burgers with crunchy batter 97
    Smoked fish kedgeree 94
    Stir-fried lemon and ginger fish 96
    Thai fish cakes 138
Flapjack, date 125
flans – see pies, flans and tarts
French onion soup 52
French peas 102
frittatas
    Potato bacon frittata 81
    Spinach, herb and feta frittatas (gluten free) 23
fritters
    Courgette and cottage cheese fritters 22
    Wheat-free corn fritters 22
fruit – see also specific fruits
    Five ways with canned fruit 112
    Fresh fruit porridge 19
    Fruit salad dessert 112

Gado gado 44
Gratin of pumpkin 108
Gravy 79
    Red wine gravy 66
Greek lamb koftas 74

ham
    Ham and mozzarella cannelloni 56
    Ham, mustard and cheese muffins 129
    Mustard chicken loaf 85
    Pea and ham soup 49
Honey and mustard salad dressing 37
Hummingbird cake 126

Ice cream 120
icings
    Lemon cream cheese icing 123
    Passionfruit icing 126
Indian butter chicken 86
Irish stew 75
Italian sandwiches 32

Jam and cream porridge 19

lamb
    Greek lamb koftas 74
    Irish stew 75
    Lamb and prune casserole 77
    Lamb chops with ginger marinade 73
    Lamb kebabs with mint sauce 74
    Lamb shanks in red wine gravy 76
    Lamb tagine 75
    Roast leg of lamb 78–9
Leek and potato soup 52
lemons

Lemon and apricot chicken 86
Lemon citron tart 116
Lemon cream cheese icing 123
Lemon sour cream cake 128
Stir-fried lemon and ginger fish 96
lentils
    Lentil tart 106
    Spicy lentil and carrot soup 50
Lime and chilli salad dressing 37
Liver and bacon 83
Louise cake 127

Mango and banana cake 124
Marinated strawberries
    and passionfruit cream 114
Melba toast 136
Meringues, chocolate and hazelnut 118
Microwave cheesy vegetables 109
Microwave muesli 20
Minestrone 48
Mini risotto balls 140
Minted peas with yoghurt and feta 102
Muesli biscuits 127
Muesli, microwave 20
Muesli squares, peanut butter 122
muffins
    Bran muffins 125
    Ham, mustard and cheese muffins 129
mushrooms
    Creamy mushrooms and bacon 21
    Chicken and mushroom egg noodles 28
    Chicken and mushroom pie 89
    Fettucine with bacon, mushrooms
        and blue cheese 55
    Mushroom soup 51
    Steak and mushroom potato top pie 64
Mushy peas 102
Mussel chowder 50
Mustard chicken loaf 85

Nachos, quick 31
Nasi goreng (Indonesian fried rice) 57
No-bake chocolate cake 122
noodles
    Five ways with noodles 28
    Pork and noodle stir-fry 84
    Spicy beef and noodle stir-fry 65
    Vietnamese noodle salad 43

Olive, tomato and cottage cheese dip 29
One pot savoury beans and rice 55
onions
    French onion soup 52
    Pumpkin and onion flan 105
    Rustic caramelised onion and tomato tarts 32
oranges
    Citrus and balsamic-glazed chicken 87
    Silverbeet, orange and haloumi salad 40
Oxtail stew 70

Paella, Spanish 95
Pancakes, banana caramel 21
Parmesan crumbed chicken 88
Passionfruit cream 114
Passionfruit icing 126
pasta
    Fettucine with bacon, mushrooms
        and blue cheese 55
    Ham and mozzarella cannelloni 56
    Pumpkin orzo salad 40

Spaghetti and meatballs 59
Spinach and salami with penne 56
Vegetable and cottage cheese lasagna 103
Pâté, chicken liver, with melba toast 136
peaches
    Easy peach crumble 112
    Peach porridge and custard 19
Peanut butter muesli squares 122
Peanut dip 29
Pear tarte tatin 119
Pears and pecorino 112
peas, dried: Pea and ham soup 49
peas, green
    Five ways with frozen peas 102
    Pea and bacon risotto 54
pies, flans and tarts, savoury
    Bacon and egg pie 34
    Chicken and mushroom pie 89
    Fish and smoked mussel pie 98
    Lentil tart 106
    Pumpkin and chicken filo pies 90
    Pumpkin and onion flan 105
    Rustic caramelised onion and tomato tarts 32
    Silverbeet and feta pie 107
    Steak and mushroom potato top pie 64
pies, flans and tarts, sweet
    Apricot tart 112
    Baked chocolate tart 115
    Lemon citron tart 116
    Pear tarte tatin 119
    Rhubarb and apple pie 118
pizzas
    Pita bread pizzas 31
    Salami pizzas 63
pork – see also bacon; ham
    Barbecue pork spare ribs 82
    Pork and noodle stir-fry 84
    Pork and prunes 81
    Pork, apricot and ginger skewers 83
Porridge 19
potatoes
    Leek and potato soup 52
    Potato bacon frittata 81
    Salami and sage potatoes 63
    Steak and mushroom potato top pie 64
Prawn toasts 134
prunes
    Devils on horseback 137
    Lamb and prune casserole 77
    Pork and prunes 81
pumpkin
    Gratin of pumpkin 108
    Pumpkin and chicken filo pies 90
    Pumpkin and onion flan 105
    Pumpkin and smoked chicken risotto 58
    Pumpkin orzo salad 40
    Spicy squash stew 110

raspberries
    Apple and raspberry frosty cream 112
    Eaton mess 117
Rhubarb and apple pie 118
rice 60–1
    Banana rice pudding 119
    Mini risotto balls 140
    Nasi goreng (Indonesian fried rice) 57
    One pot savoury beans and rice 55
    Pea and bacon risotto 54
    Pumpkin and smoked chicken risotto 58
    Salmon risotto cakes 94

Spanish paella 95
Roast beef with Yorkshire pudding 66
Roast chicken 91–2
Roast leg of lamb 78–9
Rustic caramelised onion and tomato tarts 32

salads
    Chicken and apricot salad 42
    Chickpea and beetroot salad 41
    Gado gado 44
    Grilled chicken caesar salad 45
    Pumpkin orzo salad 40
    Salami salad 63
    Silverbeet, orange and haloumi salad 40
    Tabbouleh 43
    Vietnamese noodle salad 43
    Winter roasted vegetable salad 39
salami
    Calzone 33
    Five ways with salami 63
    Italian sandwiches 32
    Spinach and salami with penne 56
salmon
    Smoked salmon and goat's cheese roll-ups 134
    Salmon puffs 139
    Salmon risotto cakes 94
    Thai-seasoned salmon steaks 97
Sandwiches, Italian 32
Satays, mixed 139
sauces
    Chilli dipping sauce 133
    Mint sauce 74
    Mustard sauce 67
    Satay sauce 135
    Tomato sauce 103
    Yoghurt sauce 137
sausages
    Spanish sausage casserole 80
scones, wholemeal yoghurt 129
Scottish porridge 19
seafood – see also fish
    Creamy garlic mussels 96
    Easy seafood chowder 48
    Fish and smoked mussel pie 98
    Mixed satays 139
    Mussel chowder 50
    Prawn toasts 134
    Spanish paella 95
Shortbread 128
Silverbeet and feta pie 107
Silverbeet, orange and haloumi salad 40
slices – see biscuits and slices
Smoked fish kedgeree 94
Smoked salmon and goat's cheese roll-ups 134
Smoothies, yoghurt 20
snacks, healthy 35
soups 47
    Creamy corn chowder 49
    Creamy tomato and basil soup 51
    Easy seafood chowder 48
    French onion soup 52
    Leek and potato soup 52
    Minestrone 48
    Mushroom soup 51
    Mussel chowder 50
    Pea and ham soup 49
    Quick Vietnamese soup 28
    Spicy lentil and carrot soup 50
Sour cream and relish dip 29

Soy and sesame salad dressing 37
Spaghetti and meatballs 59
Spanish paella 95
Spanish sausage casserole 80
Spicy baked beans 24
Spicy beef and noodle stir-fry 65
Spicy lentil and carrot soup 50
Spicy squash stew 110
Spinach and salami with penne 56
Spinach, herb and feta frittatas (gluten free) 23
Spring vegetables in rice wrappers 133
Squash stew, spicy 110
steak 71–2 – see also beef
    Steak and mushroom potato top pie 64
Stir-fried lemon and ginger fish 96
Strawberries, marinated,
    and passionfruit cream 114
Sweet potato vegetable curry 104

Tabbouleh 43
tarts – see pies and tarts
Thai chicken curry 90
Thai chicken meatballs with satay sauce 135
Thai fish cakes 138
Thai red beef curry 69
Thai-seasoned salmon steaks 97
Tiramisu, easy 117
tofu
    Tofu and sweet chilli egg noodles 28
    Veggie tofu burgers 105
tomatoes
    Boston baked beans 82
    Cheese tomato and bread pudding 106
    Creamy tomato and basil soup 51
    One pot savoury beans and rice 55
    Rustic caramelised onion and tomato tarts 32
    Spaghetti and meatballs 59
    Spanish paella 95
    Tomato and avocado salsa bruschetta 23
    Tomato chilli noodles 28
    Tomato, olive and cottage cheese dip 29
    Tomato sauce 103
Tostadas 34

vegetables – see also salads;
    and specific vegetables
    Beef and vegetable casserole 68
    Gado gado 44
    Microwave cheesy vegetables 109
    Spring vegetables in rice wrappers 133
    Sweet potato vegetable curry 104
    Vegetable and cottage cheese lasagna 103
    Veggie tofu burgers 105
    Winter roasted vegetable salad 39
    Vietnamese noodle salad 43
    Vinaigrette, basic 37

Wheat-free corn fritters 22
Wholemeal yoghurt scones 129
Winter roasted vegetable salad 39

yoghurt
    Fruit salad dessert 112
    Minted peas with yoghurt and feta 102
    Wholemeal yoghurt scones 129
    Yoghurt dressing 41
    Yoghurt sauce 137
    Yoghurt smoothies 20
Yorkshire pudding 66

5 BUDGET FRIENDLY family dinners
SERVES 4

Spring Meal Plans

Use this meal plan and shopping list to create 5 tasty family dinners – easy and cheap, in season veges, zero food waste and nutritionally balanced!

MON

Vietnamese style noodle salad with peppered chicken

TUES

Korean style rice bowl

WED

Soft tacos with crispy fish

THURS

Paprika spiced tomato and lentil pasta

FRI

Friday night egg fried rice

Thursday

Paprika spiced tomato and lentil pasta

A vegetarian take on Hungarian paprikash, a great comfort food highlighting the sweet, peppery and subtle earthy flavours of paprika.

Prep time: 10 minutes **Cooking time:** 30 minutes

Serves: 4 **Skill level:** Easy as

Ingredients

300g pasta of choice

1 tablespoon oil, divided

1 large onion*, diced

2 cloves garlic, finely chopped or 1 teaspoon crushed garlic

300g mushrooms*, sliced

1 tablespoon paprika

400g can chopped tomatoes

250ml (1 cup) water

400g can lentils, drained and rinsed

2 large carrots, grated

1 teaspoon sugar (optional)

300g (2 cups) frozen peas*

300g frozen spinach* defrosted

Salt and pepper, to taste

Method

1. Cook pasta according to packet instructions.
2. Heat oil in a deep frying pan or skillet on the stove over medium-high heat, sauté onions until they become soft. Add garlic and mushrooms and cook until fragrant and the mushrooms are cooked. Add paprika, mix and cook for about a minute.
3. Turn the heat to high and carefully pour canned tomatoes, water, lentils, carrots, and sugar (if using) into the pan, bring to a simmer.
4. Add peas and spinach to the pan once the sauce has slightly thickened, simmer for another 2 minutes. Test taste, adding salt and pepper to taste.
5. Portion pasta into bowls and top with paprika spiced tomato and lentil sauce.

Cooking tips:

- There will be extra dry pasta, store this in an airtight container in a cool place.

Adapt it:

- Use frozen corn instead of peas if you prefer.
- Paprika can be swapped for mixed herbs.
- Serve with grated cheese.

Kid-friendly alternatives:

- Use minimal salt when cooking.
- Add extra peas, corn or frozen mixed veg instead of spinach if preferred.

Leftovers:

- The cooked pasta and sauce can be frozen separately. Or can also be eaten for lunch the next day.

* Some ingredients will be used across more than one meal in a week. These ingredients are all marked with a * so you know not to use all of the ingredient in one meal.

Tuesday

Korean-style rice bowl

Korean inspired, a Bibimbap-style rice bowl is traditionally served in a hot stone bowl and topped with seasoned meat and a combination of fresh and cooked veges.

Prep time: 15 minutes **Cooking time:** 25 minutes

 Serves: 4

 Skill level: Easy as

Ingredients

Note that this recipe cooks double the amount of rice as half is used in the Friday meal, cook 300g rice if only cooking this dish.

400g beef schnitzel, sliced
1 tablespoon soy sauce
1 teaspoon vinegar
2 teaspoons sugar
2 cloves garlic, grated or 1 teaspoon crushed garlic
½ teaspoon ground pepper or a generous amount of cracked pepper
600g medium grain rice *see note in the cooking tips below
1 tablespoon oil
250g mushrooms*
100g bean sprouts* or other sprouts
2 large carrots*, sliced into matchsticks
400g frozen spinach*, defrosted
150g (1 cup) frozen green peas*
½ bunch spring onions*, sliced thinly with the green and white part separated
½ teaspoon sesame oil (optional)
Salt, to taste

Method

1. Combine beef with soy sauce, vinegar, sugar, garlic, and pepper in a bowl and let it sit for at least 5 minutes.
2. Cook rice according to package instructions.
3. Heat oil in a frying pan on the stove over high heat, fry beef in batches and set aside.
4. Cook mushrooms, bean sprouts, carrots, spinach, peas, and the white part of the spring onion in the same pan. Once cooked add sesame oil if using and salt, to taste. Set aside.
5. To serve, scoop half the rice into bowls and top with cooked beef and veges, ending with a generous sprinkle of the remaining green parts of the spring onions.

Cooking tips:

- This recipe cooks double the amount of rice needed for this meal, cool the rice you don't eat and place in the fridge and use the remaining rice to make the Friday night egg fried rice.
- Bibimbap is also commonly served with a fried egg on top – if desired you can add this to your meal.

Adapt it:

- Use brown rice instead of white to add more fibre to this meal.
- The beef can be swapped for chicken, pork, lamb, fish, tofu, tempeh or another plant-based protein alternative.
- Mix up the veges if you like based on whatever you enjoy the most.

Kid-friendly alternatives:

- Avoid adding extra salt and use reduced salt soy sauce

Leftovers:

- Eat for lunch the next day.

* Some ingredients will be used across more than one meal in a week.
These ingredients are all marked with a * so you know not to use all of the ingredient in one meal.

Week 2 Menu

Monday	Vietnamese style noodle salad with peppered chicken
Tuesday	Korean style rice bowl
Wednesday	Soft tacos with crispy fish
Thursday	Paprika spiced tomato and lentil pasta
Friday	Friday night egg fried rice

Introduction

- The recipes in this meal plan are designed for spring as they use seasonal produce.

- The meals are designed to be zero food waste. All the shopping list ingredients you buy should be used by the end of the week. For some meals you may have leftovers and the recipe will tell you whether they're suitable for freezing or are best eaten the next day.

- The shopping list tells you the ingredients to buy for the week. The pantry staples lists other ingredients you will need but are likely to have in your fridge or pantry already. Before going shopping check you have the staple ingredients and check your fridge, freezer and pantry as you may already have some of the ingredients on the list.

- If there is an ingredient you or your family doesn't like, swap it with one you'll all enjoy and avoid waste.

- These 5 meals are designed to use in-season fruit and veges. Fruit and vege growing conditions and pricing vary throughout each season, so choose cheaper in season fresh, or frozen substitutes if a particular item is unseasonably expensive.

More ways to save:

- Buy supermarket brands like Pams and Value

- Stock up on specials of items you use a lot. Buy meat on special and freeze it if you have space.

- Make substitutions – if a suitable product or cut of meat is on special, substitute it for the one in your recipe. Look at the New World weekly mailer while writing your shopping list!

Protein balance based on nutrition guidelines recommendations

These recipes are based on current nutritional guidelines. Varying the type of protein in your evening meals can help you get a good balance of nutrients. A good guide is to aim to have fish once or twice a week, chicken with the skin removed once or twice a week, lean red meat twice a week, one egg-based meal, and one vegetarian meal. The 'adapt it' tips show you how to change up the recipe to enhance the nutritional content.

Weekly tips

- We recommend cooking the Korean style rice bowl before the fried rice as cooled leftover rice is best for making the fried rice. Other than that, you can cook the recipes in any order you like.

- It is best to cool the rice down quickly by spreading it out on a clean tray or wide plate to stop the steaming then transfer into a container and place in the fridge or freezer.

- The bean sprouts used in these recipes can be substituted with your favourite sprouts or omit them if your family doesn't like them. To keep bean sprouts fresh and crisp, rinse them and transfer into a container, fill with cold water, cover with a lid, and keep in the fridge. Change this water every 1-2 days.

- There will be some leftover dry pasta at the end of this week, store this in a sealed container in a cool place and cook another day.

* Some ingredients will be used across more than one meal in a week. These ingredients are all marked with a * so you know not to use all of the ingredient in one meal.

5 BUDGET FRIENDLY family dinners

SERVES 4

Summer Meal Plans

MON — Red curry stir fried noodles

Use this meal plan and shopping list to create 5 tasty family dinners – easy and cheap, in season veges, zero food waste and nutritionally balanced!

TUES — Lamb kofta

WED — Satay salad

THURS — Tuna empanadas

FRI — Friday night sliders

Thursday

Tuna empanadas

Our simple take on a classic Spanish recipe – our empanadas use seasonal veggies and tuna. Ideal for lunch boxes, or serve with a seasonal salad for tasty family dinner.

Prep time: 15 minutes **Cooking time:** 35 minutes

Serves: 4 **Skill level:** Easy as

Ingredients

TUNA EMPANADAS

1 tablespoon oil

1 onion*, finely diced

2 capsicums*, thinly sliced or cut into small cubes

3 cloves garlic, grated or 1 ½ teaspoons crushed garlic

1 tablespoon paprika

1 cob fresh corn kernels* or 1 cup frozen corn kernels

170g tomato paste

425g canned tuna in Springwater, drained

Salt and pepper, to taste

780g flaky puff pastry sheets, defrosted

1 egg, beaten (optional)

SUMMER SALAD

1 tablespoon olive oil

1 teaspoon Dijon mustard or 2 teaspoons wholegrain mustard

Salt and pepper, to taste

1/3 head lettuce*, sliced

½ cucumber*, sliced

½ pack or bunch radish*, sliced

Method

1. Heat oil in a frying pan on the stove over medium high heat. Sauté onions and capsicum for 5-10 minutes until softened. Add garlic and fry for 1-2 minutes until fragrant, mix in paprika and corn.

2. Stir in the tomato paste and heat through. Remove from heat, gently mix in the tuna, test taste and season with salt and pepper.

3. Heat oven to 210°C bake or 190°C fan bake and grease a baking tray.

4. Prepare a small bowl of cool water, set aside.

5. Cut pastry sheets into quarters, place tablespoonfuls of mixture evenly into middle of the pastry squares, lightly brush edges with water using pastry brush or your fingers. Fold diagonally to form a triangle, seal edges with a fork, place on the baking tray. Repeat process until all mixture and pastry have been used up. Brush tops with egg, if desired.

6. Bake for 25-30 minutes, or until the pastry is golden brown and cooked through.

7. Prepare salad as the empanadas bake. Mix olive oil, mustard, salt and pepper in a bowl, add remaining salad ingredients and toss to coat in the dressing.

Cooking tips:

- If you prefer another dressing, or have an existing dressing in your fridge or pantry, use that in the salad instead.

Adapt it:

- Swap paprika with your favourite spices or sauce mix.
- For protein substitutions use minced chicken, beef or pork, prawns, salmon fresh or canned, or plant-based mince.

Leftover tips:

- Eat for lunch the next day or freeze the empanadas.

* Some ingredients will be used across more than one meal in a week. These ingredients are all marked with a * so you know not to use all of the ingredient in one meal.

*Some ingredients will be used across more than one meal in a week.
These ingredients are all marked with a * so you know not to use all of the ingredient in one meal.

Tuesday

Lamb koftas with roasted veggies

A spiced mince dish inspired by Middle Eastern cuisine, serve these lamb koftas with a side of delicious roast vegetables and a big dollop of hummus or tzatziki.

 Prep time: 10 minutes   **Cooking time:** 30 minutes

 **Serves:** 4   **Skill level:** Easy as

Ingredients

KOFTAS
- 500g lamb mince
- 1 onion*, finely diced
- 2 cloves garlic, grated or 1 teaspoon crushed garlic
- 1 teaspoon ground coriander
- 2 teaspoons garam masala
- ½ teaspoon salt
- Pepper, to taste
- 2 tablespoons oil, for frying

ROASTED VEGGIES
- 2 courgettes*, cut into chunks
- 1 eggplant, cut into chunks
- 2 capsicums*, cut into chunks or slices
- 1 tablespoon oil
- 2 cloves garlic, grated or 1 teaspoon crushed garlic
- ½ teaspoon salt
- Pepper, to taste

TO SERVE
- 8 pack pita bread, ideally wholemeal
- 1/3 cup your choice of sauce or spread e.g. hummus, tzatziki, chutney

Method

1. Combine the first seven ingredients in a bowl and set aside.
2. Heat oven to 180°C or bake or 160°C fan bake.
3. Toss the vegetables, oil, and seasoning ingredients together in a roasting tray or large baking dish. Bake for 20-30 minutes or until cooked.
4. Heat oil in a large frying pan on the stove over medium high heat.
5. Roll mince mixture into patties, balls or logs as the oil is heating up. Cook in batches until all the mince is cooked.
6. Heat the pita bread if desired, cut in half.
7. To serve, spread your choice of sauce or spread inside the pita bread. Or cut the pita bread into quarters and portion the veggies and kofta onto plates or wide bowls and top with your choice of sauce or spread.

Cooking tips:
- This recipe can be cooked on a barbecue, follow the same preparation steps explained in the method and cook on a preheated barbecue.

Adapt it:
- Add red onion into the roasted veggie mix if you like.
- Fresh finely chopped coriander or parsley added into the kofta mix is also a nice addition.
- For protein substitutions use chicken or beef mince, swap the kofta mix for falafels (most veggie minces are unlikely to stick together enough).

Leftovers
- Eat for lunch the next day. Any leftover kofta can be frozen.

Week 2 Menu

Monday	Red curry stir fried noodles
Tuesday	Lamb kofta
Wednesday	Satay salad
Thursday	Tuna empanadas
Friday	Friday night sliders

Introduction

- The recipes in this meal plan are designed for summer as they use seasonal produce.
- The meals are designed to be zero food waste. All the shopping list ingredients you buy should be used by the end of the week. For some meals you may have leftovers and the recipe will tell you whether they're suitable for freezing or are best eaten the next day.
- The shopping list tells you the ingredients to buy for the week. The pantry staples lists other ingredients you will need but are likely to have in your fridge or pantry already. Before going shopping check you have the staple ingredients and check your fridge, freezer and pantry as you may already have some of the ingredients on the list.
- If there is an ingredient you or your family doesn't like, swap it with one you'll all enjoy and avoid waste.
- These 5 meals are designed to use in-season fruit and veges. Fruit and vege growing conditions and pricing vary throughout each season, so choose cheaper in season fresh, or frozen substitutes if a particular item is unseasonably expensive.

More ways to save:

- Buy supermarket brands like Pams and Value
- Stock up on specials of items you use a lot. Buy meat on special and freeze it if you have space.
- Make substitutions – if a suitable product or cut of meat is on special, substitute it for the one in your recipe. Look at the New World weekly mailer while writing your shopping list!

Protein balance based on nutrition guidelines recommendations

These recipes are based on current nutritional guidelines. Varying the type of protein in your evening meals can help you get a good balance of nutrients. A good guide is to aim to have fish once or twice a week, chicken with the skin removed once or twice a week, lean red meat twice a week, one egg-based meal, and one vegetarian meal. The 'adapt it' tips show you how to change up the recipe to enhance the nutritional content.

Weekly tips

- The recipes for this week can be cooked in whatever order you prefer. To keep the sliders or buns fresh, store them in the freezer and bring them out that morning to defrost.
- Beef cuts such as rump steak, stir fry, schnitzel, or other steak cuts will all work perfectly – check the weekly specials to get the best deal.
- Coconut milk is a shared ingredient. Keep it fresh by storing the remaining milk in a sealed container in the fridge.
- Red curry paste is shared between two recipes. If your family doesn't like red curry, use any tomato-based sauce to flavour the noodle stir fry, such as a pad Thai sauce. You can make a mild coconut satay sauce for the satay salad by leaving out the red curry paste.
- Nectarines are used as part of the corn slaw with the sliders – you can use another stone fruit or swap to an apple or pear instead.

* Some ingredients will be used across more than one meal in a week. These ingredients are all marked with a * so you know not to use all of the ingredient in one meal.

BBQ Vegetable Salad with Dill & Feta Yoghurt

BBQ Vegetable Salad with Dill & Feta Yoghurt

It's time to crank up the barbie and enjoy this perfectly barbequed vegetable salad topped with creamy dill & feta yoghurt. Simple and easy to make this vibrant vegetarian dish is packed full of flavour and will be devoured in seconds!

 Serves: 6-8

 Prep time: 20 mins
Cooking time: 20 mins

 Skill level: Easy as

Ingredients

2 capsicums, cut into chunks

2 courgette, cut into quarters lengthwise

1 eggplant, cut into thick rounds

1 fennel, trimmed and quartered

1 red onion, cut into wedges

Olive oil

1 large rosemary sprigs

1 cup Greek yoghurt

1 tbsp freshly chopped dill, plus extra for garnish

50g feta cheese

1 lemon

4 vine tomatoes, diced

¼ red onion, finely diced

2 tbsp capers

Method

1. Preheat a BBQ or grill to a high heat. Place the vegetables in a bowl and drizzle lightly with olive oil, and sprinkle over the chopped rosemary. Season with salt and pepper, then place onto the BBQ and cook until charred and tender (time will vary according to vegetable type).

2. To make the dressing, mix together the Greek yoghurt, dill, feta cheese and the juice of ½ a lemon. Season to taste and set aside.

3. Arrange the warm vegetables on a platter, then spoon the yoghurt sauce over the vegetables.

4. In a bowl, toss together the cherry tomatoes, red onion and capers. Drizzle with olive oil, then season to taste. Sprinkle over the salad, then garnish with additional fresh dill and lemon wedges. Serve and enjoy.

newworld.co.nz/recipes

 newworldnz

Curried Butterfly BBQ Chicken

Curried Butterfly BBQ Chicken

Dive into the season of sunny opportunities with this curried butterfly BBQ chicken. Marinated in a delicious blend of Greek yoghurt, fresh coriander, curry powder and citrus, it's a scrumptious meal worth repeating. Serve with a side of warm pita bread and a chopped summer salad of your choice. We suggest a leafy salad mix with microgreens and purple basil leaves.

 Serves: 6

 Prep time: 15 mins + marinating
Cooking time: 1 hour 10 mins

 Skill level: Easy as

Ingredients

- 1.5kg butterfly chicken
- ¾ cup Greek yoghurt
- ½ cup fresh coriander, roughly chopped
- 2 tbsp curry powder
- 2 lemons
- 3 cloves garlic, minced
- 3 courgette, sliced

Method

1. Pat the chicken dry with a paper towel and place in a large dish.
2. To make the yoghurt marinade, in a small bowl, mix together yoghurt, coriander, curry powder, the zest and juice of one lemon, garlic, salt and pepper. Spread the marinade all over the chicken, then place in the fridge to marinade for a few hours or overnight.
3. Preheat your BBQ to medium high heat and brush with oil. Place the chicken skin side down and BBQ for 5-10 minutes or until golden brown and lightly charred. Turn the chicken over and reduce the heat to low. Cover and cook for a further 40-50 minutes or until the chicken is cooked through. Set aside to rest for 10 minutes.
4. Toss the courgette with a drizzle of olive oil, salt and pepper. Grill for 3-5 minutes on each side or until charred and tender.
5. Cut the remaining lemon into wedges and serve with the rested chicken and grilled courgette.

Top Tip

- This curried butterfly chicken can also be cooked in the oven. Preheat your oven to 200°C and place the chicken skin side up on a lined roasting dish or tray. Bake for 1 hour or until cooked through, covering with foil after 20 minutes. Set aside to rest for 10 minutes before serving. Follow the steps above to prepare the courgette, then place on a baking tray and roast for 15 minutes or until tender.

newworld.co.nz/recipes

 newworldnz

Cornflaked French Toast with Fruits

Cornflaked French Toast with Fruits

Crisp, crunchy and absolutely scrumptious to devour, our cornflaked French toast is the ultimate start to any morning! Easy to make and oh so delicious, be sure to serve your French toast with your favourite summer fruits and a generous drizzle of maple syrup.

 Serves: 4

 Prep time: 10 mins
Cooking time: 15 mins

 Skill level: Easy as

Ingredients

- 3 eggs
- ½ cup milk
- ½ cup cream
- ¼ cup caster sugar
- 1 tsp vanilla extract
- ¼ tsp cinnamon
- 8 slices thick white bread
- 2 cups cornflakes
- 50g butter
- ½ cup mascarpone or yoghurt
- Canadian maple syrup, to serve
- Fresh fruits of your choice, to serve

Method

1. In a bowl, whisk together the eggs, milk, cream, caster sugar, vanilla and cinnamon until fully incorporated. Dip each slice of bread into the egg mixture, then coat both sides in cornflakes.

2. Bring a non-stick frying pan to a medium heat with some butter, then lay 2-3 slices into the pan (or as many as can fit). Pan fry the French toast for 2-3 minutes each side, or until golden brown and crispy.

3. Set the cooked French toast aside and repeat with the remaining slices; adding more butter to the pan as needed.

4. Serve the French toast alongside a dollop of mascarpone, fresh fruit of your choice and a generous drizzle of maple syrup. Serve immediately and enjoy.

newworld.co.nz/recipes

newworldnz

Nectarine & Haloumi Bruschetta

Nectarine & Haloumi Bruschetta

Beautiful summer stone fruit sings in this delectable bruschetta! Caramelised nectarines and squeaky haloumi pair perfectly on top of your favourite toasted bread, dressed with fresh tomatoes and basil for the ultimate hassle-free dish.

 Serves: 4-8

 Prep time: 10 mins
Cooking time: 15 mins

 Skill level: Easy as

Ingredients

100g cherry tomatoes, diced

Handful fresh basil leaves, shredded

1 tbsp finely diced red onion

1 small clove garlic, finely chopped

1 lemon

6-8 slices crusty bread of your choice

Olive oil

3 nectarines, cut into wedges

200g block haloumi cheese, cut into ½ cm thick slices

Balsamic glaze or vinegar, to finish

Additional fresh basil leaves, to garnish

Method

1. In a bowl, combine the diced cherry tomatoes, basil leaves, red onion, garlic and the juice of ½ the lemon. Drizzle lightly with olive oil, season with salt and pepper, then stir to combine. Set aside.

2. Place a grill pan over a medium to high heat. Drizzle the bread slices with olive oil, then grill on both sides until golden brown. Remove from the heat, then set aside.

3. Lower the grill pan to a low to medium heat. Drizzle the nectarine wedges with olive oil, then place onto the grill and cook for 2-3 minutes each side or until caramelised. Set aside.

4. Finally, lightly oil the haloumi slices and cook for a minute on each side, or until golden brown in colour. Remove from the heat and squeeze over the remaining lemon juice.

5. To assemble the bruschetta, arrange the nectarine and haloumi slices on top of the toasted bread. Spoon the dressed tomatoes over the top, then drizzle with balsamic and finish with fresh basil. Serve immediately and enjoy.

Top Tip

- Consider yourself more of a peach fan? You can always use peaches instead for a delicious substitute.

newworld.co.nz/recipes

 newworldnz

Easy 10-Minute Couscous

Easy 10-Minute Couscous

You can't go wrong with a 10-minute meal like this Mediterranean-inspired couscous packed with seasonal vegetables. This light and easy meal is perfect for busy summer evenings and will have your tamariki gobbling up their veggies. Serve on a bed of baby spinach for an extra serving of greens.

Serves: 4

Prep time: 5 mins
Cooking time: 5 mins

Skill level: Easy as

V

Ingredients

1 ½ cups couscous

1 tbsp Moroccan spice

1 onion, diced

2 cloves garlic, minced

1 eggplant, cut into 1.5cm cubes

2 courgettes, thinly sliced

1 red capsicum, cut into thin 2cm strips

1 can (400g) chickpeas, drained

½ cup parsley leaves, chopped

Method

1. In a large bowl, mix the couscous and Moroccan spice with one and a half cups of boiling water. Cover and leave to absorb.

2. Meanwhile, bring a large pan to medium-high heat with a drizzle of olive oil. Sauté the onion and garlic for a minute. Add the eggplant, courgette and capsicum and sauté for 3-4 minutes or until the vegetables have softened.

3. Fluff the couscous with a fork, mix through the sautéed vegetables and chickpeas, and season with salt and pepper to taste.

4. Spoon onto plates and finish with a sprinkling of chopped parsley.

Top Tip

- Take this veggie-packed couscous up a notch by serving it with a delightfully creamy feta yoghurt. Simply mix one cup of natural Greek yoghurt, seventy grams of crumbled feta and the juice of half a lemon juice in a small bowl. Season with salt and pepper to taste and finish your dish with a generous dollop.

newworld.co.nz/recipes

newworldnz

Monday

Red curry stir-fried noodles

Everyone will love this fragrant noodle recipe! Packed with flavour and easy to make, this beef and mushroom stir-fry dish is also easy to re-heat for lunch the next day.

Prep time: 10 minutes   **Cooking time:** 30 minutes

Serves: 4   **Skill level:** Easy as

Ingredients

250g rice noodles

2 tablespoons oil, divided

500g beef rump steak, sliced or stir fry beef

1 onion*, finely diced or sliced

½ jar red curry paste*

250g mushrooms

2 courgettes*, sliced

200ml coconut milk*

1 carrot*, sliced thinly or into match sticks

1/3 cabbage*, sliced thinly

Pepper, to taste

Method

1. Cook noodles according to packet instructions. Set aside.
2. Heat oil in a wok, deep frying pan or skillet on the stove over high heat.
3. Sear the beef for 1-2 minutes in batches and transfer onto a plate, set aside.
4. Reduce heat to medium high adding more oil to the pan if needed, sauté onions until softened. Add half the jar of red curry paste and fry for around 2 minutes while stirring occasionally until it is very fragrant.
5. Add mushrooms and courgettes, stir fry until cooked to your liking. Mix in coconut milk and bring to a simmer.
6. Stir through cooked noodles, carrots, cabbage, and beef, cover with a lid and heat through to cook while mixing occasionally. Add small amounts of water if it is getting too dry. Test taste, season with salt and pepper if needed.

Cooking tips:

- If omitting the red curry paste from this recipe you can make a tomato-based pad thai sauce instead.

Adapt it:

- You can use egg noodles if you prefer.
- For protein substitutions use chicken, tofu, tempeh, prawns, fish, quorn, plant-based meat alternatives.

Leftovers

- Eat for lunch the next day.

* Some ingredients will be used across more than one meal in a week. These ingredients are all marked with a * so you know not to use all of the ingredient in one meal.

Wednesday

Satay salad

Our quick and easy take on gado-gado, an Indonesian salad with peanut sauce. With a flavour-packed, creamy peanut sauce and topped with eggs and crispy tofu, the whole whānau will love it!

Prep time: 15 minutes **Cooking time:** 15 minutes
Serves: 4 **Skill level:** Easy as

Ingredients

- 6 eggs
- 2 tablespoons oil
- 250g firm tofu, cut into squares or rectangles
- 2/3 head lettuce*, roughly chopped
- 1 capsicum*, sliced
- ½ cucumber*, sliced
- ½ pack or bunch radish*, thinly sliced or cut into matchsticks
- 1 large carrot*, sliced into ribbons or thin match sticks

SAUCE

- ½ jar red curry paste*
- 200ml coconut milk*
- 2 teaspoons peanut butter, smooth or crunchy

Method

1. Cook eggs whole in boiling water to your liking. About 3mins for soft-boiled or 6mins or longer for a firmer yolk. Set aside to cool then peel.
2. Heat oil in a non-stick pan over stove on high heat, cook tofu until golden brown. Remove from pan and set aside.
3. Lower heat to medium, add additional tablespoon of oil and fry curry paste in the same pan for about 1-2mins, until fragrant. Carefully pour in the coconut milk and stir.
4. Add peanut butter and bring to a simmer at reduced heat for about 5mins to thicken, stir occasionally. Test taste, adding more peanut butter, soy sauce or seasoning as needed. Transfer into a bowl.
5. Toss veggies in a large bowl. Cut eggs into halves or quarters.
6. To serve, portion fresh salad into wide bowls or plates, top with egg, tofu, and drizzle the sauce over top or serve on the side.

Cooking tips:

- Substitute peanut butter with 2 tablespoons tahini for a nut free alternative.
- For a fuller meal you can add rice noodles.
- To save time on the day the eggs can be hardboiled beforehand and stored in the fridge.

Adapt it:

- To reduce the salt, opt for no added salt peanut butter.
- To make a mild coconut satay sauce omit the red curry paste and increase the peanut butter quantity to ¾ cup.
- Use chicken as a protein substitution.

Leftover tips:

- Eat for lunch the next day.

* Some ingredients will be used across more than one meal in a week. These ingredients are all marked with a * so you know not to use all of the ingredient in one meal.

Friday

Friday night BBQ sliders

For a Friday night treat, gather the whānau to devour these pulled chicken sliders! The BBQ chicken pairs perfectly with a zesty corn and stone fruit slaw.

Prep time: 15 minutes   **Cooking time:** 25 minutes

Serves: 4   **Skill level:** Easy as

Ingredients

PULLED CHICKEN

2 teaspoons oil

2 teaspoons smoked paprika

300g-400g chicken breast

2 tablespoons barbecue sauce

CORN AND STONE FRUIT SLAW

2 cobs fresh corn kernels* or 2 cups frozen corn kernels

1/8 cabbage* or remaining cabbage, sliced thinly

1 carrot*, grated

2 large nectarines, cut into small cubes or thin slices

1 tablespoon sour cream, yoghurt, or mayonnaise

1 teaspoon mustard

Salt and pepper, to taste

½ cup nuts and seeds (if desired)

TO SERVE

8 pack sliders or buns

Method

1. Poach chicken breast for about 10 minutes or until cooked, leave to cool slightly and shred using two forks or your fingers if it is cool enough to handle.

2. Boil corn in a pot to heat through and cook, drain. Combine the slaw ingredients in a large bowl, set aside.

3. Heat oil in a frying pan on the stove over medium heat. Add smoked paprika and shredded chicken and stir.

4. Add the barbecue sauce and mix to evenly coat the chicken. Test taste, adding more spice, salt, and pepper, or teaspoonfuls of barbecue sauce.

5. Toast the buns or heat them in the oven.

6. To serve, scoop generous spoonsful of the slaw onto the bottom half of the bun, top with the BBQ chicken and the top half of the bun. Serve any additional slaw on the side.

Cooking tips:

- To save time poach the chicken a day or two before hand, store in a sealed container in the fridge and shred just before cooking. You can substitute the smoked paprika with any of your favourite spice mixes. You can also use any sauce you like instead of BBQ sauce.

Adapt it:

- As a vegetarian option swap out the chicken for two cans of young green jackfruit. For protein substitutions use shredded beef, lamb, or pork, grilled or pan-fried fish.

Leftover tips:

- Eat for lunch the next day.

* Some ingredients will be used across more than one meal in a week. These ingredients are all marked with a * so you know not to use all of the ingredient in one meal.

Shopping List

Produce
- [ ] 3 Onions
- [ ] 250g Mushrooms
- [ ] 4 Courgettes
- [ ] 3 Carrots
- [ ] ½ Cabbage
- [ ] 5 Capsicums
- [ ] 1 Lettuce
- [ ] 1 Cucumber
- [ ] 200g Radishes
- [ ] 1 Eggplant
- [ ] 3 Corn cobs
- [ ] 2 Nectarines

Grocery
- [ ] 250g Rice noodles
- [ ] 160g Red curry paste

- [ ] 170g Tomato paste
- [ ] 425g Canned tuna
- [ ] 6 Eggs
- [ ] 400ml Coconut milk
- [ ] 8 pack Pita bread
- [ ] 8 pack Sliders/buns

Butchery
- [ ] 500g Beef, stir fry or rump steak
- [ ] 500g Lamb mince
- [ ] 400g Skinless chicken breast

Chilled
- [ ] 250g Firm tofu

Frozen
- [ ] 780g Flaky puff pastry sheets

Pantry Staples*

- [ ] Oil, for frying
- [ ] Olive oil
- [ ] Salt
- [ ] Pepper
- [ ] Garlic – fresh cloves or crushed
- [ ] Paprika – smoked or sweet
- [ ] Soy sauce, coconut aminos / other alternative
- [ ] Peanut butter

- [ ] Ground coriander
- [ ] Garam masala
- [ ] Barbecue sauce
- [ ] Sour cream, mayonnaise, or yoghurt
- [ ] Mustard – Dijon or wholegrain
- [ ] Your favourite sauce – hummus, tzatziki, chutney
- [ ] Nuts and seeds (optional)
- [ ] Egg (optional addition)

*These items are usually found in your pantry and not included in the budget.

For more meal plans to make shopping & cooking easy and affordable visit newworld.co.nz/meal-plans

Monday

Vietnamese style noodle salad with peppered chicken

Fresh and light, this easy chicken salad is elevated by combining seared peppered chicken with seasonal veges and topping with a zesty Vietnamese-style dressing.

Prep time: 15 minutes **Cooking time:** 20 minutes

Serves: 4 **Skill level:** Easy as

Ingredients

Peppered chicken

400g skinless chicken breast, sliced into strips

2 teaspoons cracked pepper

1 tablespoon oil

NOODLE SALAD

250g vermicelli noodles

1 red onion, thinly sliced

½ cucumber*, sliced into sticks

100g bean sprouts* or other sprouts

2 large carrots, cut into thin matchsticks

1 large capsicum, sliced

150g (½ packet) mesclun salad*

DRESSING

Juice and rind of 1 ½ lemons*

2 teaspoons sweet chilli sauce

1 teaspoon fish sauce or ½ teaspoon soy sauce

1 clove garlic, grated or ½ teaspoon crushed garlic

Method

1. Mix the chicken and pepper in a bowl. Heat a frying pan on the stove over high heat, add oil to the pan and fry chicken in batches. Set aside.
2. Cook noodles according to package instructions and portion into bowls or wide plates.
3. Evenly distribute the fresh salad ingredients over the cooked noodles.
4. Mix all the dressing ingredients in a bowl, test taste adding more sweet chilli or fish sauce if needed. Drizzle sauce evenly over the noodle salad.
5. Top salad with cooked chicken and serve.

Cooking tips:
- Try using different seasonings such as lemongrass or honey soy to flavour your choice of protein.

Adapt it:
- You can switch the chicken for pork, beef, lamb, white fish, salmon, tofu, tempeh, or another protein alternative.

Kid-friendly alternatives:
- For younger children, vermicelli noodles can be a choking hazard, so swap for thicker rice or egg noodles and chop after cooking if needed.
- Use reduced salt soy sauce.
- Adapt the salad veges based on what your kids will eat.

Leftovers:
- Eat for lunch the next day.

* Some ingredients will be used across more than one meal in a week. These ingredients are all marked with a * so you know not to use all of the ingredient in one meal.

Wednesday

Soft tacos with crispy fish

Looking for a quick and easy meal to feed the whānau? Our crumbed fish tacos hit the spot for a nutritious, simple and delicious lunch or dinner.

Prep time: 15 minutes **Cooking time:** 20 minutes

Serves: 4 **Skill level:** Easy as

Method

1. Cook fish fillets according to packet instructions.
2. Prepare salad ingredients while the fish cooks by combining the mesclun salad, grated carrot, sliced cucumber, red onion, and capsicum in a large bowl. Add lemon zest and squeeze the juice over the salad, toss to coat and set aside.
3. Heat wraps according to packet instructions, if desired.

To assemble

- Place wrap on a plate and in any order add salad, fish, and sauce. Or place all the elements in the middle of the table for everyone to make their own taco.

Cooking tips:

- For extra crunch, roti can also be used for this dish instead of wraps.
- Wraps most commonly come in packets of 8, so if you have any left over, keep them for another meal or freeze.

Adapt it:

- The fish can be swapped for chicken, beef, lamb, pork, fish, tofu, tempeh, or another plant-based protein alternative.
- Use whatever salad veges you enjoy.

Leftovers:

- Eat for lunch the next day.

Ingredients

500g crumbed frozen fish fillets
150g (½ packet) mesclun salad*
2 large carrots*, grated
½ cucumber*, sliced thinly
1 red onion, thinly sliced
1 large capsicum, thinly sliced
Zest and juice of ½ lemon*
4–6 wholemeal wraps
Your favourite sauce, spread, or dip (optional)

* Some ingredients will be used across more than one meal in a week.
These ingredients are all marked with a * so you know not to use all of the ingredient in one meal.

Friday

Friday night egg fried rice

Inspired by Yakimeshi, a Japanese style fried rice, our vegetarian dish is loaded with veges and easy to whip up for a Friday night in!

 Prep time: 10 minutes   **Cooking time:** 20 minutes

 Serves: 4   **Skill level:** Easy as

Ingredients

2 tablespoons butter or oil, divided

6 eggs, beaten

1 large onion*, finely diced

1 leek, thinly sliced, white and green parts included

2 cloves garlic, grated or 1 teaspoon minced garlic

2 capsicums, cubed or thinly sliced

300g (2 cups) frozen green peas*

2 tablespoons soy sauce

Pepper, to taste

4 cups cooked medium grain rice* (or remaining rice from the Korean rice bowl meal)

300g frozen spinach*, defrosted

½ bunch spring onions*, green and white parts thinly sliced

1 teaspoon sesame oil (optional)

Method

1. Heat a deep frying pan, a skillet or a wok on the stove over high heat, add 1 tablespoon butter or oil and cook the eggs. As they begin to set break it up into smaller pieces or cook as one large pancake and cut into slices. Set aside.

2. Reduce heat to medium high, add remaining butter or oil and sauté onions until they become soft. Add leek and garlic, then fry for about 5 minutes.

3. Turn up the heat to high, add capsicums, peas, soy sauce, and pepper, stir fry for 1-2 minutes.

4. Add rice and heat through, mix in spinach and spring onions, mix to combine, and test taste. Add a little more soy sauce and/or pepper as desired. Stir through cooked eggs.

5. Finish with a drizzle of sesame oil (if using), briefly stir through and serve.

Cooking tips:

- This recipe works best with cooled rice. If you have not cooked the rice already, cook 300g of medium grain rice.
- You can add any leftover cooked meat and veges to this dish if you have any.

Adapt it:

- Use brown rice to boost the fibre of this meal.
- You can add an extra onion instead of the leek if preferred.
- Use 8 eggs in total if you have larger appetites.
- You can add cooked chicken, leftover meat or pan fried tofu or tempeh to boost the protein.
- Sprinkle with chopped peanuts or sesame seeds.

Kid-friendly alternatives:

- Swap spinach for extra frozen peas or corn if preferred.

---

* Some ingredients will be used across more than one meal in a week.
  These ingredients are all marked with a * so you know not to use all of the ingredient in one meal.

Shopping List

Produce
- [ ] 2 Red onions
- [ ] 1 Cucumber
- [ ] 200g Mung bean sprouts
- [ ] 8 Carrots
- [ ] 4 Capsicums
- [ ] 300g Mesclun salad
- [ ] 2 Lemons
- [ ] 550g Mushrooms
- [ ] 1 Bunch spring onions
- [ ] 2 Onions
- [ ] 1 Leek

Butchery
- [ ] 400g Skinless chicken breast
- [ ] 400g Beef schnitzel

Grocery
- [ ] 250g Vermicelli noodles
- [ ] 1kg Medium grain rice
- [ ] 8 Pack wholemeal wrap
- [ ] 500g Dry pasta
- [ ] 400g Can chopped tomatoes
- [ ] 400g Can lentils
- [ ] 6 Eggs

Frozen
- [ ] 500g Crumbed fish fillets
- [ ] 750g Peas
- [ ] 1kg Spinach

Pantry Staples*

- [ ] Salt
- [ ] Pepper
- [ ] Oil
- [ ] Sweet chilli sauce
- [ ] Soy sauce
- [ ] Garlic – fresh bulbs or crushed
- [ ] Vinegar
- [ ] Sugar
- [ ] Paprika
- [ ] Your favourite sauce or spread
- [ ] Fish sauce (optional)
- [ ] Sesame oil (optional)
- [ ] Butter (optional)

*These items are usually found in your pantry and not included in the budget.

For more meal plans to make shopping & cooking easy and affordable visit newworld.co.nz/meal-plans